MW01601988

Que® Quick Reference Series

Q&A™ Quick Reference

Bryan Pfaffenberger

Que Corporation
Carmel, Indiana

This book is based on Q&A Version 3.0.

Que Quick Reference Series

The *Que Quick Reference Series* is a portable resource of essential microcomputer knowledge. Whether you are a new or experienced user, you can rely on the high-quality information contained in these convenient guides.

Drawing on the experience of many of Que's best-selling authors, the *Que Quick Reference Series* helps you easily access important program information.

Now it's easy to look up often-used commands and functions for 1-2-3, dBASE IV, WordPerfect 5, Microsoft Word 5, and MS-DOS, as well as programming information for C, Turbo Pascal, and QuickBASIC 4.

Use the *Que Quick Reference Series* as a compact alternative to confusing and complicated traditional documentation.

The *Que Quick Reference Series* includes these titles:

Publishing Director

Lloyd J. Short

Product Director

Karen A. Bluestein

Editor

Cheryl S. Robinson

Technical Editor

Paul Dughi

Proofreaders

Jodi Jensen
Diana Moore

Indexer

Joelyn Gifford

Trademark Acknowledgments

dBASE, dBASE III Plus, and dBASE IV are registered trademarks of Ashton-Tate Corporation.

1-2-3, Lotus, Symphony, and VisiCalc are registered trademarks of Lotus Development Corporation.

PFS, PFS:FILE, PFS:GRAPH, PFS:REPORT, and PFS:WRITE are registered trademarks of Software Publishing Corporation.

Q&A is a trademark of Symantec Corporation.

Table of Contents

Introduction

Q & A Quick Reference includes the quick reference information you need to work with Q&A's five modules: File, Report, Write, Intelligent Assistant, and Utilities. This book includes the most frequently used reference information you need to design and use databases, generate reports, create documents, and use Q&A's English-language data retrieval capabilities.

Because it is a quick reference, this book is not intended to replace the extensive documentation and tutorials included with Q&A. This book highlights the most frequently used information and reference material required to work quickly and efficiently with Q&A. Not covered are some advanced features that few Q&A users employ, such as the program's extensive networking capabilities (However, you will find extensive coverage of Q&A's advanced and form programming capabilities, which are useful for virtually every Q&A user.) Moreover, this book does not attempt to teach you Q&A concepts and methods with keystroke-by-keystroke tutorials; it's for review and reference.

If you're new to Q&A, there's no better way to supplement the Q&A knowledge contained in this book than to obtain a copy of *Using Q&A*, 2nd Ed., by David P. Ewing and Bill Langenes (Que Corporation, 1988). This well-written book walks you step-by-step to Q&A mastery, and includes extensive coverage of advanced features such as networking and importing non-Q&A databases.

Q&A Quick Reference is divided into sections by tasks, command names, and topics. One section, for example, is called **Search/Update**. It covers the procedures you use to retrieve and update forms from a File database. Additional, relevant information is found in **Search Options**, a reference section that surveys the codes you can use to tailor Q&A searches with precision.

Now you can put essential information at your fingertips with *Q&A Quick Reference*—and the entire Que Quick Reference series.

Q&A Applications

Q&A includes an excellent database module, an easy-to-use report generator, a word processing module that is fully integrated with the database facilities, and a sophisticated English-language retrieval system called the Intelligent Assistant.

Q&A includes the following applications:

- **File** is a flat-file database management program. You design your own forms. Then you add data to the forms, producing a database—a collection of records (filled-in forms). You can retrieve the forms you want to see, and then sort, edit, update, or even delete the forms.

- **Report** is an easy-to-use module for printing the information in your database. You can use Q&A's built-in report formats, or create your own, just as easily as you created your form design.

- **Write** is a word processing program that is fully integrated with Q&A's database capabilities. Use Write to create letters, memos, and reports. It includes many advanced functions such as search and replace, headers and footers, and multiple columns. You can create reports that incorporate reports generated by File and enhance them with Lotus 1-2-3 or Symphony spreadsheets and graphics.

- **Intelligent Assistant** translates English queries into instructions for data retrieval and report generation. Intelligent Assistant doesn't really understand English, and to get the module working at peak efficiency, you must "train" it to understand the words you use.

- **Utilities** includes facilities for importing and exporting data, installing your printer, using DOS, choosing default directories, and recovering damaged databases.

Hints for Using This Book

Because Q&A consists of five separate modules all provided in one package, this Quick Reference includes a subhead under each boxed header that refers you to a specific Q&A application. The subhead tells you which module to choose to achieve the desired result.

For example, you see the word *FILE* under Assign Access Rights. This subhead tells you that you must choose File from the Main Menu to control access rights.

Conventions used in this book

As you read this book, keep the following conventions in mind.

To choose commands from menus, use the up- and down-arrow keys to highlight the command you want. You also can press the letter shown in blue, as in the following example:

Choose **S**et global defaults from the Utilities Menu.

All keys that you press appear in boldfaced blue type.

The material in this book is extensively cross-referenced. When you see a command name or topic printed in italic, turn to the section with that title. Here's an example:

See *Information Types* for a list of information type codes.

Q&A makes extensive use of function keys, and often uses them in combination with the Shift, Ctrl, and Alt keys. You need not memorize the meanings of these keys, however.

Because Q&A accomplishes so many different tasks, the meaning of the function keys changes as you move from module to module within the program. To help you remember the functions of these keys, many of this book's entries contain summaries of the function keys relevant to a specific command or module.

Menu bypassing shortcuts

Q&A's menu structure helps you navigate through the program. After you learn the structure of the program, however, you may want to use the menu bypassing shortcuts. These shortcuts bypass the menus and take you from one function to another.

Key	Result
Adding Data	
F7	Retrieve Spec Screen
Shift-F9	Bypass menu (Format, Restrict Spec, Initial Values Spec, Speedup Spec, Lookup Table, Help Spec, Change Palette Spec)
Updating Data	
Ctrl-F6	Add data
F7	Retrieve Spec
Shift-F9	Bypass menu (Format, Restrict Spec, Initial Values Spec, Speedup Spec, Lookup Table, Help Spec, Change Palette Spec)
Customizing Form Design	
Ctrl-F6	Add data
F7	Retrieve Spec
Printing Reports	
F2	Print Options
Shift-F9	Bypass menu (Retrieve Spec, Column/Sort Spec, Derived Column Spec, Print Options, Define Page)
Printing Forms	
F2	Print Options
Shift-F9	Bypass menu (Retrieve Spec, Column/Sort Spec, Derived Column Spec, Print Options, Define Page)
Editing Documents	
F2	Print Options
Alt-F8	Print Mailing Labels
Ctrl-F6	Define Page
Shift-F8	Save document
Ctrl-F8	Export document to ASCII

COMMAND REFERENCE

Add Data

FILE

Purpose

Displays a new, blank form so that you can add new information to the database.

Notes

Use Search/Update to add data to partially filled out forms.

If you created a keyword field, remember to separate the keywords with semicolons.

When you design a data file, you give each field an Information Type. If you try to enter alphanumeric characters in a number field, the keys you press have no effect. For other information types, Q&A checks what you typed after you exited the field. If the data entered does not conform to the information type, you see an error message such as `This doesn't look like a yes/no value. Please verify`. You see a similar message when you violate a restriction spec you created. See *Restrict Values*.

To automatically enter the current date in a field, press **Ctrl-F5**. To automatically enter the current time in a field, press **Alt-F5**.

To add data

1. Choose **F**ile from the Main Menu.

2. Choose **A**dd Data.

3. Type the name of the data file, or press **Enter** to see a list of available data files.

   You may now add information. Use the Backspace, Delete, F4, or Shift-F4 keys to edit text as you type. See *Editing Keys*.

4. Press **Tab** or **Enter** to move the cursor to the next field.

You also can use the cursor-movement keys to navigate around the form.

If you make many mistakes and prefer to start over, press **F3** and choose **Y**es to delete the form permanently.

5. Press **F10** to save the form and display a new form, or press **Shift-F10** to save the form and exit.

To print a displayed form

1. Press **F2**.

2. Choose **P**rint Options, if you want.

3. Press **F10** to start printing.

To print all forms added

1. Press **Ctrl-Home**.

2. Press **Ctrl-F2**.

3. Press **F10**.

Add Data Function Keys

Key	*Function*
F1	Displays Help screen.
F2	Prints current form.
Shift-F2	Displays Macro Menu.
Ctrl-F2	Prints from current form to end of stack.
F3	Deletes current form.
F4	Deletes from cursor to end of field.
Shift-F4	Deletes all characters in field.
F5	Copies current field from previous record.
Shift-F5	Copies previously viewed record.
Ctrl-F5	Inserts current date.
Alt-F5	Inserts current time.
F6	Displays up to 17 records in a five-column table.

F7	Activates the Search/Update function.
F8	Calculates.
Shift-F8	Sets Calc mode.
Ctrl-F8	Resets @NUMBER.
F9	Saves and displays previous record.
Shift-F9	Displays Customize Spec screen.
F10	Saves and displays a new, blank form.
Shift-F10	Saves record and exits.
Esc	Returns you to File Menu.

Advanced Lessons

ASSISTANT

Purpose

Teaches Intelligent Assistant more words.

Note

Use Advanced Lessons only after you use Basic Lessons. The choices you make affect the current database.

To identify name fields

1. Choose Intelligent Assistant from the Main Menu.

2. Choose **T**each Me about Your Database.

3. Press **4** to choose Which Fields Contain People's Names.

4. After placing the cursor in the first field containing a person's name, press **1** to identify the person, and type an abbreviation after the number to identify which part of the name the field contains.

   Use the following abbreviations: **W** (whole name), **F** (first name), **T** (title), **M** (middle name), **L** (last name), **S** (suffix, such as degree).

5. Press **Tab** to place additional codes in other fields containing this person's name.

   Each individual has just one number. If you typed **1L** to identify the first person's last name, type **1F** to identify the field containing the same person's first name.

6. Repeat Steps 2 and 3 for each additional person named on the form.

7. Press **F10** to save your work and continue.

8. When prompted, type words or phrases that describe the person whose name you identified.

9. Press **F10**.

To identify units of measure fields

1. Choose Intelligent Assistant from the Main Menu.

2. Choose **T**each Me about Your Database.

3. Press **2** to select the Units of measure option from the Advanced Lessons Menu.

4. Type the name of the measurement unit, if you used one.

5. Press **F8** to select the next field.

6. Repeat Steps 2 and 3 until you identify all the fields that contain units of measure.

7. Press **F10** to continue.

To teach adjectives used for comparison

1. Choose Intelligent Assistant from the Main Menu.

2. Choose **T**each Me about Your Database.

3. Press **3** to choose the Advanced vocabulary: adjectives option.

4. To use adjectives to compare the data in this field, type the high value (such as *expensive*) and the low value (such as *cheap*). If not, skip this step.

   Do not type the comparison suffixes -*er* and -*est*.

   Intelligent Assistant knows the following bases (as well as their comparative and superlative derivatives): much, many (more, most), big (bigger, biggest), great (greater, greatest), large (larger, largest), high (higher, highest), low (lower, lowest), few (fewer, fewest) , small (smaller, smallest), little (littler, littlest), less, least, above, below, under, maximum (max), minimum (min), top, and bottom.

5. Press **F8** to select the next field.

6. Repeat Steps 2 and 3 until you identify all fields that you can compare using adjectives.

7. Press **F10** to continue.

To teach verbs you associate with fields

1. Press **4** to choose the Advanced vocabulary: verbs option.

2. If you want to use verbs to describe an action connected with data in this field, type **verb**. If not, skip this step.

   Examples include "When was Smith *hired*?" "What final grade did Jones *achieve*?"

   If the verb is irregular, you must type the irregular forms you will use.

   Intelligent Assistant knows verbs that describe the program's built-in actions, such as count, show, give, and present.

3. Press **F8** to select the next field.

4. Repeat Steps 2 and 3 until you identify all the action fields.

5. Press **F10** to continue.

Ask Me To Do Something

ASSISTANT

Purpose

Receives a request in English to retrieve information, add new information, change information, perform calculations, produce reports, and create synonyms.

Notes

Use Basic Lessons and Advanced Lessons before using this command.

In general you can ask the Intelligent Assistant to perform any database functions. The following examples are typical questions and commands you can ask, but it may be necessary to teach the program many additional words.

- **What is**..? What is the highest grade for Essay No. 4? What are the highest grades for Essay No. 1 and Essay No. 2?

- **Who**..? Who has the highest grade for Essay No. 4? Who has not handed in Essay No. 3 on time?

- **How Many..?** How many students handed in Essay No. 3 on time? How many students handed in 0 essays on time?

- **Where**..? Where did the students with above average final grades go to high school?

- **Show me**... Show me a list of all the students whose final grade is above average, sorted by major. Tell me the average grade, maximum grade, and minimum grade for Essay No. 3.

- **Get**... Show me all the forms for students who have not handed in papers on time. Get the forms for students who did not hand in Paper No. 3 on time.

- **Change**... Change Deborah Smith's Essay No. 3 grade from 2.75 to 3.0. Change the weight of the final exam to 15, and change the weight of Essay No. 4 to 10.

- **Delete**... Erase Jim Smith's form. Delete any forms with all grades blank.

When you ask Intelligent Assistant to display data, the program displays or prints all the columns you identified in Basic Lessons. You can limit the display of data by adding the codes WNIC ("With No Identifying Columns"), WNRC ("With No Restriction Columns"), and WNEC ("With No Extra Columns"). You add the codes at the end of the query or command.

To display the data in a Yes/No field, you must type the word field after the field name.

To ask Intelligent Assistant to do something

1. Choose **A**sk Me to Do Something from the Assistant Menu.

2. Type the name of the database you want to customize.

3. Type the request in the Request box and press **Enter**.

   If Assistant cannot understand one of the words you used, it asks for help. You can edit the word, add the word to Q&A's vocabulary, display or change the vocabulary, or choose to ignore the problem and tell Assistant to go ahead.

4. Choose **Y**es to confirm the request and carry out the action.

   If you want, press **F2** to print the results of the query or command.

To add words to Assistant's vocabulary

1. Choose **A**sk Me to Do Something from the Assistant Menu.

2. Type the name of the database.

3. Press **F8**.

4. Indicate whether the word or phrase you want to add is a **W**ord, a **F**ield name, a **S**ynonym, a **V**erb, or **O**ther.

To change the name of the Intelligent Assistant

1. Choose **A**sk Me to Do Something from the Assistant Menu.

2. Type the name of any database.

3. Type **I dub thee** *name* and press **Enter**.

Function Keys in Ask Me To Do Something

Key	Function
F1	How to ask
F4	Delete word
Shift-F4	Delete line
F6	See vocabulary
Shift-F7	Restore previous request
F8	Teach words

Assign Access Rights

FILE

Purpose

Defines access privileges and passwords.

Notes

Access protection can prevent unauthorized persons from reading sensitive records. In addition, the database administrator can determine the level of access.

When you define access control, your choices affect the current database. Other databases lack protection unless you activate them and choose Assign Access Rights.

You can define the following access levels:

- **Administrative Rights** includes the right to change the Access Control screen and determine the access rights of other users.

- **Change Form Design** enables the user to redesign and customize the database design.

- **Change Report Design** enables you to design or modify an existing report.

- **Data Access Level** contains two options. The Read and Write option allows the user to add, update, or delete data. The Read only option prevents the user from making any change to the data.

The first Access Control screen should be filled out by the database administrator. After you select a User ID and password and quit Q&A, you must supply this information the next time you access this database.

You need enter your user ID and password only once a session by pressing **F6** at the Main Menu. Alternatively, Q&A prompts you for this information if you attempt to open a restricted database.

To assign access rights

1. Choose **F**ile from the Main Menu.

2. Choose **D**esign File.

3. Type the name of the database you want to customize and press **Enter**.

4. Choose **C**ustomize a File.

5. Choose **A**ssign Access Rights.

6. Type your User ID and press **Enter**.

   Use something familiar, such as your first name. You may type up to 20 characters.

7. Type a password and press **Enter**.

   You may type up to 10 characters.

8. Press **Tab** to select the next Access Rights field, and choose the option you want for this user.

9. Repeat Step 8 until you finish choosing Access Rights for this user.

10. To add a new user, press **Ctrl-F6** and fill out the form.

    To view the forms, press **F9** to display the previous form and **F10** to display the next form. To delete a form, press **F3**.

11. Press **Shift-F10** to save the forms and return to the Access Menu.

To change a password

1. Start Q&A and access a restricted database.

2. When the password box appears, type your user ID and current password.

3. Press **F8**.

4. Type your new password.

5. Check the password carefully for typographical or other errors. Correct any errors.

6. Press **F10**.

To delete Access Control for a user

1. Choose **F**ile from the Main Menu.

2. Choose **D**esign File.

3. Type the name of the database you want to customize and press **Enter**.

4. Choose **C**ustomize a File.

5. Choose **A**ssign Access Rights.

6. Choose **A**ssign Access Rights from the Access Menu.

   You see the first Access Control form.

7. Press **F10** or **F9** to find the Access Control form you want to delete.

8. Press **F3**.

9. Choose **Y**es and press **Esc** to return to the Access Menu.

Backup

FILE

Purpose

Creates an exact image copy of a database.

Notes

Use Backup to make copies of your databases every time you add or update records. If your original database becomes corrupted due to a system crash, power surge, or a disk problem, you can use the backup copy.

Backup makes an exact copy of your database, including all the gaps and other inefficiencies that mount up as a database is used. To make a new working copy of your database that compacts unused space, see *Copy*.

If you want to backup a database that is larger than your floppy drive's storage capacity, use a tape backup unit, a larger-capacity floppy drive, or a backup program that can distribute a file over two or more floppies.

A database consists of two files, a .DTF and an .IDX file. Backup copies both files.

To copy the database design without copying records, see *Copy*.

To backup a database

1. Choose **B**ackup from the File Menu.

2. Type the name of the database you want to back up, and press **Enter**.

3. Type the name of the destination file and press **Enter**.

Basic Lessons ══════════════

ASSISTANT

Purpose

Teaches Intelligent Assistant information about your database.

Note

Before using Intelligent Assistant for the first time for a given database, choose **T**each Me About Your Database from the Assistant Menu.

To teach Intelligent Assistant what this database is about

1. Press **1** to select What This Database is About from the Basic Lessons Menu.

2. Type a word or phrase that completes the statement, "Each form contains information about a particular _____."

   Type as many synonyms as you can. Press **Enter** after each synonym.

3. Press **F10** to save the words.

To teach Intelligent Assistant which fields to include in reports

1. Press **2** to select Which Fields Identify a Form from the Basic Lessons Menu.

2. Specify the order in which you want the fields to appear.

3. Press **F10** to continue.

To teach Intelligent Assistant which fields contain locations

1. Select option **3** from the Basic Lessons Menu.

2. Specify the first location field you want to appear in reports by pressing **1**, specify the second location field by pressing **2**, and so on.

   If there are no location fields, skip this step.

3. Press **F10**.

To teach Intelligent Assistant about alternate field names

1. Select option **4** from the Basic Lessons Menu.

2. Type synonyms for the first field label.

   For example, you can enter the synonyms "surname," "proper name," and "last" for a field titled "Last Name."

3. Press **F8**.

4. Repeat Steps 2 and 3 until you identify synonyms for all the field labels.

5. Press **F10**.

Block Operations

WRITE

Purpose

Marks a block of text for copying, deleting, moving, or printing.

Note

You can move text from one document to another using the Clipboard feature.

To copy a block of text

1. Place the cursor on the first character of the block you want copied.

2. Press **F5**.

3. Highlight the text you want to copy.

   You also can press a letter key (A-Z or a-z) to select the text up to the next occurrence of the letter.

4. Press **F10**.

5. Move the cursor to the location you want the copied text to appear.

6. Press **F10** to copy the block.

   To make another copy of the block, press **Shift-F7**.

To copy text to a new document

1. Place the cursor on the first character of the block you want copied.

2. Press **Ctrl-F5**.

3. Highlight the text you want to copy.

   You also can press a letter key (A-Z or a-z) to select all the text up to the next occurrence of the letter.

4. Press **F10**.

5. Type the name of the new file to which you want the block copied.

6. Press **Enter** to copy the block to the file.

To move text within a document

1. Place the cursor on the first character of the block you want moved.

2. Press **Shift-F5**.

3. Highlight all the text you want to move.

   You also can press a letter key (A-Z or a-z) to select all the text up to the next occurrence of the letter.

4. Press **F10**.

5. Move the cursor to the location you want the text to appear.

6. Press **F10** to copy the block.

   To make another copy of the block you just moved, press **Shift-F7**.

To move text to a new document

1. Place the cursor on the first character of the block you want moved.

2. Press **Ctrl-F5**.

3. Highlight the text you want to move.

   You also can press a letter key (A-Z or a-z) to select all the text up to the next occurrence of the letter.

4. Press **F10**.

5. Type the name of the new file to which you want the block moved.

6. Press **Enter** to copy the block to the file.

To delete a block of text

1. Place the cursor on the first character of the block you want deleted.

2. Press **F3**.

3. Highlight the text you want to delete.

   You also can press a letter key (A-Z or a-z) to select all the text up to the next occurrence of the letter.

4. Press **F10**.

To restore the deletion, press **Shift-F7** before you press any other keys.

To print a block of text

1. Turn on and select your printer.

2. Place the cursor on the first character of the block you want printed.

3. Press **Ctrl-F2**.

4. Highlight the text you want to delete.

You also can press a letter key (A-Z or a-z) to select all the text up to the next occurrence of the letter.

5. Press **F10**.

Calculations

WRITE

Purpose

Performs arithmetic and statistical operations.

Notes

You can total, average, count, multiply, and divide on numbers entered in a column or a row. Q&A treats numbers preceded by a minus sign (-) or typed with parentheses as negative. To subtract, type a negative number and choose **A**dd.

The number of decimal places is determined by the number of decimal places in the numbers you typed, except that Write adds two decimal places for averaging and division operations.

To perform calculations

1. Type the numbers in a column or row using flush right or decimal tab alignment.

Do not leave blank lines between the numbers if you are performing calculations on a column.

2. Position the cursor on the last number of the column or after the last number of the row.

3. Press **Alt-F9**.

4. Choose **T**otal, **A**verage, **C**ount, **M**ultiply, or **D**ivide.

5. Place the cursor where you want the result.

6. Press **F10**.

Centering a Line

FILE, WRITE

Purpose

Centers a line of text on a page.

To center a line

1. In Design File or Type/Edit, type the line.

2. Place the cursor anywhere in the line.

3. Press **F8**.

4. Choose **C**enter Line and press **Enter**.

To uncenter a line

1. Place the cursor anywhere in the line.

2. Press **F8**.

4. Choose **U**ncenter Line and press **Enter**.

Change Palette

FILE

Purpose

Provides options for the display of foreground and background display attributes.

Note

Because the choice you make is saved with the current database, you can choose distinctive palettes for each database.

To view and change the palette options

1. Choose **F**ile from the Main Menu.

2. Choose **D**esign File.

3. Type the name of the database you want to customize and press **Enter**.

4. Choose **C**ustomize a File.

5. Choose **C**hange Palette.

6. Press **F8** to see the next palette or **F6** to see the previous palette.

   To see how text looks, you can type in the fields. Q&A does not save these characters.

7. When you have the palette you prefer, press **F10** to return to the Customize Menu.

Checking Spelling

WRITE

Purpose

Checks the current document for words that do not match Write's dictionary. Also searches for duplicated words (such as "the the").

Notes

If Write encounters a word that does not match its dictionary, you see the Spelling menu. You can choose from the following options:

- **L**ist possible spellings displays up to seven possible correct spellings of the word. You may select the word and press **Enter** to place the correct spelling in your document.

- **I**gnore word and continue skips this and all additional occurrences of the word. Choose this option for seldom-used proper nouns (such as street names) and other correctly-spelled words that you do not want to add to your Personal Dictionary.

- **A**dd to dictionary & continue adds the word to your Personal Dictionary and continues the spelling check. Choose this option for proper nouns or technical terms that are likely to recur in your writing.

- Add to dictionary and **S**top adds the word to your Personal Dictionary and cancels the spelling check.

- **E**dit word and recheck permits you to edit the word manually. Type the correct spelling and press **Enter**. Write checks the spelling of the correction.

To spell check an entire document

1. In Type/Edit, press **Ctrl-Home** to position the cursor at the beginning of the document.

2. Press **Shift-F1**.

   The program highlights any word that does not match the dictionary and displays the Spelling menu.

3. Choose an option from the Spelling menu.

4. Repeat Step 3 until you see the message
   `Spelling check completed.`

To check the spelling of a single word

1. Place the cursor on the word.

2. Press **Ctrl-F1**.

3. Choose an option from the Spelling menu.

To edit your Personal Dictionary

1. Choose **G**et from the Write Menu.

2. Type the file name **qapers.dct**.

3. When you see the Import Document menu, choose **A**SCII and press **Enter**.

Although you can correct, delete, or add words, you must keep the words in alphabetical order, one to a line. Enter new words in lowercase letters unless they are proper nouns.

You must save the personal dictionary as ASCII text.

4. Press **Esc**.

5. Choose **U**tilities.

6. Choose **E**xport to ASCII.

7. Choose **S**tandard ASCII.

8. Press **Enter**.

Clear

WRITE

Purpose

Clears the current document from memory.

To clear memory

Choose **C**lear from the Write Menu and press **Enter**.

If you have not saved the current document you see a warning message. Press **N** to cancel the command or press **Y** to continue.

Clipboard

WRITE

Purpose

Moves text from one document to another.

Note

To move text within a document, see *Block Operations*.

To move text from one document to another

1. Place the cursor at the beginning of the text you want to move.

   Make sure that Q&A is in the Overwrite mode. If you see `Insert` on the message line, press **Ins**.

2. Press **Shift-F5**.

3. Highlight the text you want to move.

4. Press **F10**.

5. Move the cursor back to the first character of the text you just added to the Clipboard, and press **F10** again.

6. Save the document by pressing **Shift-F8**.

7. Press **Esc**.

8. Choose **G**et from the Write Menu.

9. Type the name of the document to which you want to move the text.

   To see a list of available documents, press the spacebar to clear the line and press **Enter**.

10. Press **Enter**.

11. Move the cursor to the place you want the text to appear.

12. Press **Shift-F7**.

Column/Sort Spec Codes

REPORT

Purpose

Enables advanced report features.

Notes

You use the Column/Sort Spec Codes when you design or redesign a report format. See *Design/Redesign a Report Format* for details.

See *Derived Columns* for additional report calculation options.

Q&A's Column/Sort Spec Codes

Code	Explanation
A	Prints column average at bottom of column.
AB	Breaks and does subcalculations when first letter changes.
AS	Sorts in ascending order.
C	Prints count of entries at bottom of column.
C	Displays money with commas.
CS	Cancels subcalculations.
DB	Breaks and does subcalculations when day changes.
D*n*	Uses data format *n* (type a number from 1-20).
DS	Sorts in descending order.
H*n*	Uses time format *n* (type a number from 1 to 3).
JC	Formats text center.
JL	Formats text left justified.
JR	Formats text right justified.
M	Formats in money format.
MAX	Prints maximum value at bottom of column.
MB	Breaks and does subcalculations when month changes.
MIN	Prints minimum value at bottom of column.
N*n*	Uses *n* decimal places.
P	Forces new page when column break occurs.
R	Repeats values.
SA	Prints subaverages at column breaks.
SC	Prints subcounts at column breaks.
SMAX	Prints maximum value at column breaks.
SMIN	Prints minimum value at column breaks.
ST	Prints subtotals at column breaks.

T	Prints column total at bottom of column.
T	Formats as text.
TR	Truncates to fit.
U	Formats text uppercase.
WC	Displays numerical amounts without commas.
YB	Breaks and does subcalculations when year changes.

Conditional Statements

FILE

Purpose

Executes a programming statement only if a specified condition is met.

Notes

You create the conditional statement the same way you create other statements; see *Programming Statements* for information.

An IF/THEN statement executes an instruction if a condition is fulfilled. If not, Q&A does nothing. Here is a valid IF/THEN statement:

#10: IF #4 = "Y" THEN #12 = #8 * #6

This statement says if Field #4 contains the text 'Y,' then multiply the value in Field #8 by the value in Field #6 and place the result in Field #12.

An IF/THEN/ELSE statement executes an instruction if a condition is fulfilled. If not, Q&A executes the second instruction. Here is a valid IF/THEN/ELSE statement:

**#10: IF #8 < 10 THEN #12 = 50 ELSE
#12 = 100**

This statement says if Field #4 contains a value that is less than 10, then place the value 50 in Field # 12. Otherwise, place the value 100 in Field #12.

You may use the following logical operators in conditional statements to construct more complex conditions:

- **AND** requires that both conditions be true. Here is an IF/THEN statement that employs the AND operator:

  #10: IF #8 = "Y" AND #10 = "Y"
     THEN #12=100

  If Field #8 contains "Y" *and* Field #10 contains "Y," then place the value 100 in Field #12. The value 100 appears in Field #12 *only* if both conditions are true.

- **OR** requires that only one condition be true. Here is an IF/THEN statement that employs the OR operator:

  #10: IF #8 = "Y" OR #10 = "Y" THEN #12=100

  If Field #8 contains "Y" or if Field #10 contains "Y," then place the value 100 in Field #12. The value 100 appears in Field #12 if only one of the fields meets the test.

- **NOT** requires that a condition be false. Here is an IF/THEN statement that employs the NOT operator:

  #10: IF #8 = "Y" NOT #10 = "Y"
     THEN #12=100

  If Field #8 contains "Y," and as long as Field #10 contains *anything other than* "Y," then place the value 100 in Field #12. The value 100 appears in Field #12 *only* if both conditions are true—that is, Field #8 *must* contain "Y" and Field #10 *must* contain something other than "Y."

You can create multiple conditional statements within a field by linking the statements with semicolons. You also can nest conditional statements. To do so, use BEGIN and END to mark the beginning of the series of statements. (Use the curly bracket { instead of BEGIN and } instead of END.) You must write a nested statement on one or more lines in sequence.

If you plan to insert complex programming statements into a field, design (or redesign) the field so that it is a multiple-line field. That way, you will have ample room to write the programming statement.

To create the conditional statement

1. Choose **F**ile from the Main Menu.

2. Choose **D**esign File.

3. Type the name of the data file.

4. Press **Enter**.

5. Choose **C**ustomize a File.

6. Press **Enter** to confirm the file name.

7. Choose **P**rogram Form.

   You see the Program Spec screen.

8. Add Field ID numbers to any fields you will reference in your statement.

   See *Field ID Numbers* for more information.

9. Place the cursor in the field in which you want the conditional statement to appear.

10. Type a new field ID number (such as #110) followed by a colon.

11. Type the IF/THEN or IF/THEN/ELSE statement.

    Carefully follow the preceding examples given to make sure that you write the statement with the correct syntax.

12. Press **F10** to save your statement and return to the File menu.

Copy

FILE

Purpose

Creates a new database using the database design, the data, and the instructions you gave the Intelligent Assistant.

Notes

To make an exact backup copy of your database for
security purposes, the Backup option is faster to use than
Copy. Use Copy when you want to copy the database
design, the database design and selected records, or
some but not all of the fields.

A database you use frequently becomes less efficient,
both in terms of disk space and retrieval time. When you
use Backup, Q&A makes an exact image copy of the
original—including all the gaps and inefficient
arrangements that slow retrieval time and eat up disk
space. When you copy all the records with Copy,
however, Q&A makes a more efficient version of the
database.

When copying forms, you copy from the *source
database* to the *destination database*.

You can copy your database in these five ways:

- Copy Design Only copies the form design and all
  customization options you have chosen, but no data
  records and no Intelligent Assistant information. If
  you have not used Intelligent Assistant, choose this
  option because it is faster.

- Copy Design with Intelligent Assistant copies the
  form design and all customization options you have
  chosen. This option also copies the information you
  have taught Intelligent Assistant about the data
  base.

- Copy Selected Forms copies the form design first to
  create the destination database. The destination
  database's form design is exactly the same as the
  source database's form design. Then you use what
  amounts to a Search/Update procedure to retrieve
  the forms you want to copy to the new database. If
  you want, you can sort the source database so that
  the records in the destination database will always
  appear in sorted order.

- Compact the Database copies all the records and
  creates a more efficient version of the original
  database. This copy is not made for backup

purposes; because the destination database is more efficient, you will use it instead of the source database.

- Copy Selected Fields to a New Database Design creates a new destination database form design containing the fields you want in the new database. The names and custom formats of these fields must exactly match the fields that appear in the source database. However, you don't have to use all the fields. You use this procedure when you want to omit some of the fields in the source database.

To copy the design only

1. Choose Copy from the Form Menu.

2. Type the name of the data file.

   To see a list of available databases, press the spacebar to clear the line and press Enter.

3. Choose Copy Design Only.

4. Type a new data file name.

5. Press Enter.

To copy the design with Intelligent Assistant information

1. Choose Copy from the Form Menu.

2. Type the name of the data file.

   To see a list of available databases, press the spacebar to clear the line and press Enter.

3. Choose Copy Design with IA.

4. Type a new data file name.

5. Press Enter.

To copy selected or sorted data records from one database to another

1. Use the procedure just explained to copy the database design.

2. Choose Copy from the File Menu.

3. Type the name of the database from which you are copying and press Enter.

4. Choose Copy **S**elected Forms.

5. Type the name of the database to which you are copying and press **Enter**.

   You see a Retrieve Spec screen.

6. Use the Retrieve Spec screen to get the records you want to copy.

   You can sort the records by pressing **F8**. You also can retrieve records based on criteria you specify.

   After you sort or retrieve the records, you see the Merge Spec screen.

7. Press **F10** to copy all the fields in the order they appear on-screen.

To compact the database (copy all records)

1. Use the procedure explained above to copy the database design.

2. Choose **C**opy from the File Menu.

3. Type the name of the database that you are copying from and press **Enter**.

4. Choose Copy **S**elected Forms.

5. Type the name of the database to which you are copying and press **Enter**.

   You see a Retrieve Spec screen.

6. Press **F10** to retrieve all the records.

7. Press **F10** to copy all the fields in the order they appear on-screen.

To copy selected data fields to a new database design

1. Create a new database that contains selected fields from the source database.

   The field names, information types, and formats must match the corresponding fields from the source database.

2. Choose **A**dd data from the File Menu to display the new form.

3. Press **F2** and then **F10** to print a copy of the new form.

   Use this copy to assist you as you copy the fields.

4. Press **Esc** to return to the File Menu.

5. Choose **C**opy.

6. Type the name of the database from which you are copying and press **Enter**.

7. Choose Copy **S**elected Forms.

8. Type the name of the database to which you are copying and press **Enter**.

   You see a Retrieve Spec screen.

9. Use the Retrieve Spec screen to retrieve the records you want to copy.

   Press **F10** to retrieve all the records or use selection criteria to retrieve just some of the records.

   After you sort or retrieve the records, you see the Merge Spec screen.

10. Enter numbers in the Merge Spec fields that correspond *exactly* to the order in which the fields appear in the destination database.

    If the first field of the destination database is Last name, for example, type **1** in the Last Name field.

11. Press **F10** to start copying the fields.

Copy a Document

WRITE

Purpose

Creates a backup copy of a Write document.

To copy a document

1. Choose **W**rite from the Main Menu.

2. Choose **U**tilities.

3. Choose **C**opy a document.

4. Type the name of the document you want to copy.

5. Press **Enter**.

6. Type the name of the backup document.

7. Press **Enter**.

Counting

WRITE

Purpose

Produces a count of the number of words, lines, and paragraphs in a document.

To count words, lines, and paragraphs

From the Type/Edit screen, press **Ctrl-F3**.

Cursor Movement

FILE, WRITE

Purpose

Moves you around the screen and from screen to screen.

Key	*Cursor Effect*
Up arrow	Moves up one line or field.
Down arrow	Moves down one line or field.
Right arrow	Moves right one character.
Left arrow	Moves left one character.
Ctrl-Right arrow	Moves next word right.
Ctrl-Left arrow	Moves to previous word.
Tab	Moves to next field (File).

Shift-Tab	Moves to previous field (File).
PgUp	Moves to first character of previous screen.
PgDn	Moves to first character of next screen.
Ctrl-PgUp	Moves to first character of previous page (Write).
Ctrl-PgDn	Moves to first character of next page (Write).
Home	Moves to first character of line.
End	Moves to last character of line.
Home Home	Moves to first character of current page.
End End	Moves to last character of current page.
Ctrl-Home	Moves to first character of form (File) or document (Write).
Home Home Home	Moves to first character of form (File) or page (Write).
Home Home Home Home	Moves to first character of document (Write).
Ctrl-End	Moves to last character of form (File) or document (Write).
End End End	Moves to last character of form (File) or page (Write).
End End End End	Moves to last character of document (Write).
F9	Scrolls up (Write).
Shift-F9	Scrolls down (Write).

| Ctrl-F7 | Goes to page or line you specify. |

Cursor Movement Commands

FILE

Purpose

Automates cursor movement as you move from field to field.

Notes

Cursor movement commands are programming statements, which you create by choosing **P**rogram File from the Customize Menu. The statements affect all the records in the database when you add or update records.

To use the cursor movement commands, you must begin the programming statement with a less-than sign (<) or greater-than sign (>).

Cursor Movement Commands

Command Name	Effect
CEND	Moves the cursor to the last field in the form.
CHOME	Moves the cursor to the first field in the form.
CNEXT	Moves the cursor to the next field.
CPREV	Moves the cursor to the previous field.
GOTO field ID#	Moves the cursor to the field whose ID# matches the number in the statement.

PgDn   Moves the cursor to the first
                           field on the next page.

PgUp   Moves the cursor to the first
                           field on the previous page.

___

To create a cursor movement command

1. Choose **F**ile from the Main Menu.

2. Choose **D**esign File.

3. Type the name of the database you want to
   customize and press **Enter**.

4. Choose **C**ustomize a File.

5. Press **Enter** to confirm the file name.

6. Choose **P**rogram File.

7. If you plan to use the GOTO cursor movement
   command, enter Field ID numbers in all fields a
   programming statement references.

   Press the pound sign (#) and then a unique, whole
   number to identify the field.

8. Enter the cursor movement command in the field.

   If you want to execute the statement when you
   move the cursor into the field, begin the statement
   with a less-than sign (<). If you want to execute the
   statement when you move the cursor out of the
   field, begin the statement with a greater-than sign
   (>). Normally, you choose the greater-than sign.

   If the formula is too long to fit in the field, press **F6**
   to temporarily expand the field. Then continue
   typing the statement. Press **Tab** to exit the
   expanded field window.

9. Type the cursor movement command name.

10. Repeat Steps 8 through 10 to write additional cursor
    movement commands, if you want.

11 Press **F10** to save your programming statements
    and return to the File Menu.

Customize a File

FILE

Purpose

Provides database customization options.

Notes

You can customize a file in the following ways:

- Change the Format Options or Information Types. See *Format Values*.

- Place further restrictions on what you can type in a field. See *Restrict Values*.

- Automatically insert default or most likely values into a field to save time in data entry. See *Set Initial Values*.

- Index the fields you commonly search so that searches proceed faster. See *Speed Up Searches*.

- Include programming instructions that perform calculations and other operations on the data that appears on the form. See Program Form and Programming Statements.

- Create a table of values that Q&A consults automatically when you type data into a field. *See Edit Lookup Table*.

- Display a customized help menu to assist data entry on a field-by-information blank basis. See *Define Custom Help*.

To access the Customize Menu

1. Choose File from the Main Menu.

2. Choose Design File.

3. Type the name of the database you want to customize.

   To see a list of available databases, press the spacebar to clear the line and press Enter.

4. Press **Enter**.

5. Choose **C**ustomize a File.

6. Press **Enter** to confirm the file name.

Date and Time Display

FILE, *REPORT*

Purpose

Sets formats for display of dates and times in data
records and reports.

Date Display Formats

Code	Date Display Format
1	Jul 12, 1990
2	12 Jul 1990
3	7/12/90
4	12/7/90
5	7/12/1990
6	12/7/1990
7	07/12/90
8	12/07/90
9	07/12/1990
10	12/07/1990
11	July 12, 1990
12	12 July 1990
13	7-12-90
14	7-12-1990
15	07-12-90
16	07-12-1990
17	12.07.90
18	12.07.1990
19	1990-07-12
20	1990/07/12

Time Display Formats

Code	Time Display Formats
1	3:50 pm
2	15:50
3	15.50

Define Custom Help

FILE

Purpose

Creates a custom Help box that appears on-screen.

Notes

Once you create a custom Help box, view it by positioning the cursor in the field and pressing **F1**.

To create a custom Help box

1. Choose **F**ile from the Main Menu.

2. Choose **D**esign File.

3. Type the name of the database you want to customize.

4. Press **Enter**.

5. Choose **C**ustomize a File.

6. Choose **D**efine Custom Help.

   You see the Help Spec screen. The cursor is positioned in the first field. To select other fields, press **F8** to choose the next field or **F6** to choose the previous field.

7. Type the help message for the field in the on-screen rectangle.

8. To type another message, press **F6** or **F8** to choose the next field for which you want to create a Help box.

9. Repeat Steps 7 and 8 until you have added all the Help boxes you want.

10. Press **F10** to save your Help boxes and return to the Customize Menu.

To tell the user Help boxes are available

1. Choose **P**rogram Form from the Customize Menu.

2. Place the following statement in each field to which you added a Help statement. Make sure that you use a field ID# you have not used previously.

   ***Field ID*#:@msg"Press F1 to see a Help box for this field."**

   Make sure that you enclose the message in quotation marks.

3. Press **F10**.

To use a Help box

1. Place the cursor in the field.

2. Press **F1**.

3. To quit the Help box, press **Esc**.

Define Page

FILE, REPORT

Purpose

Defines page size, margins, characters per inch, page numbering, and headers/footers for database output.

Notes

You can define page options when you create a Print Spec or Report Format for a database (see *Design/Redesign a Print Spec* and *Design/Redesign a Report Format*). The page options you choose affect only that print spec or report format.

You also can choose new default page options for all
new print specs or report formats by choosing the Set
Global Options command in the File or Report modules.

Q&A uses the following defaults, which appear on the
Define Page screen:

- Page Width: 85 character columns (spaces)

- Page Length: 66 lines

- Left Margin: 5 character columns

- Right Margin: 80 character columns from the *left*
  edge of the page

- Top Margin: 3 lines

- Bottom Margin: 3 lines

- Characters per Inch: 10 cpi (Pica). You can choose
  12 cpi (Elite); 15 cpi (compressed printing on a
  daisywheel printer); or 17 cpi (compressed printing
  on a dot-matrix printer).

- Header: blank

- Footer: blank

You can add page numbers, current date, and current
time to headers and footers. Using special formatting
codes, you also can create a three-part header or footer,
where the first part is aligned flush left, the second part
is centered, and the third part is aligned flush right.

To add page numbers in a header or footer

1. From the Define Page screen, press **Tab** to select
   the Header or Footer area.

2. Use the cursor-movement keys to position the
   cursor where you want the page number to appear.

   Although you can create a header of up to three
   lines, most headers and footers use only one line
   (the first).

3. Press the pound sign (#).

To include date and time in a header or footer

1. From the Define Page screen, press **Tab** to select
   the Header or Footer area.

2. Use the cursor-movement keys to position the
   cursor where you want the date or time to appear.

   Although you can create a header of three lines,
   most headers and footers use only one line.

3. Type the code to display the date or time.

   You can type both codes on the same line, if you
   want, and also include page numbers.

To create a three-part header or footer

1. Place the cursor in the first column of one of the
   lines in the header or footer area.

2. Type the text or the code you want printed flush
   left.

   Omit this step if you don't want anything printed
   flush left.

3. Type an exclamation point (!).

4. Type the text or the code you want centered.

5. Type another exclamation point (!).

6. Type the text or the code you want printed flush
   right.

   Omit this step if you don't want anything printed
   flush right.

Define Page

WRITE

Purpose

Defines the page size, margins, characters per inch, and
page on which Write starts printing page numbers and
headers and footers.

Notes

To add headers or footers (including page numbers) to a
Write document, see *Edit Headers/Edit Footers*.

You can define page options when you create and save a document (see *Type/Edit*). The page options you choose affect only that print spec or report format.

The choices you make on the Define Page screen affect the current document. You also can choose new default page options for all new documents you create with Write. For more information, see *Set Global Options*.

Q&A uses the following defaults, which are shown in the Define Page screen:

- Page Width: 78 character columns

- Page Length: 66 lines

- Left Margin: 10 character columns (one inch)

- Right Margin: 68 character columns from the *left* edge of the page

- Top Margin: 6 lines

- Bottom Margin: 6 lines

- Characters per Inch: 10 cpi (Pica). You also can choose 12 cpi (Elite), 15 cpi (compressed printing on a daisywheel printer), or 17 cpi (compressed printing on a dot-matrix printer)

- Begin header/footer on page #: 1

- Begin page numbering on page #: 1

See *Temporary Margins* for information on changing the margins temporarily within a document.

To change the margins for the whole document

1. In Type/Edit, press **Ctrl-F6**.

2. Enter a new measurement for the left margin.

   You can enter inches or columns.

3. Press **Tab**.

4. Type a new measurement for the right margin.

   If you type the measurement in columns, type the number of columns from the *left* edge of the page. If you type the measurement in inches, type the measurement from the *right* edge of the page.

5. Press **Tab**.

6. Type the top margin in inches or lines, measured from the top.

7. Press **Tab**.

8. Type the bottom margin in inches or lines, measured from the bottom.

9. Press **F10**.

To suppress page numbers and headers on Page 1 of a document

1. In Type/Edit, press **Ctrl-F6**.

2. Press **Tab** to select Begin Header/Footer on Page #:, and type the page number on which you want headers or footers to begin.

3. Press **Tab** to select Begin Page Numbering with page #:, and type the page number on which you want page numbering to begin.

4. Press **F10**.

Delete

ASSISTANT, FILE, REPORT, WRITE

Purpose

Deletes characters, words, and blocks in text editing; deletes records in Search/Update (File).

Notes

Press **Shift-F7** _before doing anything else_ to restore words, lines, or blocks you just deleted. You cannot undelete text you deleted with the Backspace or Del keys.

Use the following keys to delete text as you edit.

Key	_Effect_
Backspace	Deletes character left.
Del	Deletes Character on which cursor is positioned.

F4	Deletes word.
Shift-F4	Deletes all characters in a field (File) or line (Write).
Shift-F7	Restores deletion to screen.
F3	Deletes block (Write).

To delete a form in the File module

1. Choose **S**earch/Update from the File menu.

2. Type the name of the data base and press **Enter**.

3. Use the Retrieve Spec screen to limit the search to the form you want to delete.

4. Press **F10** to display the form.

5. Press **F3**.

6. Choose **Y**es to confirm the deletion.

To delete a block of text in the Write module

1. Place the cursor on the first character of the block you want deleted.

2. Press **F3**.

3. Highlight all the text you want to delete.

   You also can press a letter key (A-Z or a-z) to select all text up to the next occurrence of the letter that you press.

4. Press **F10**.

   To restore the deletion, press **Shift-F7** *before doing anything else*.

To delete a document in the Write module

1. Choose **W**rite from the Main Menu.

2. Choose **U**tilities.

3. Choose **D**elete a document.

4. Type **Y** and press **Enter** to delete the document.

Derived Columns

REPORT

Purpose

Produces reports using information not directly available from fields on the data records.

Notes

When you produce a report, Q&A sorts the data and can perform operations such as subtotals, totals, and averages.

You can add columns to a report in which Q&A prints *derived* data. Derived data is generated by performing calculations on existing data fields in ways that are not included in the form design. For example, a form lists an employee's monthly salary and the number of tax exemptions claimed, but it does not compute the amount of tax to be withheld. This computation can be accomplished with a derived column.

When you define a derived column, you tell Q&A to compute figures listed on two regular report columns. To do so, you must write a formula. You can use Operators and column ID numbers. Be careful to observe rules of precedence (see *Operators*) and use parentheses if necessary.

In the formulas you create, you can use Summary Functions that reference the totals and subtotals of other columns in the report. You also can use the Lookup functions, @LOOKUP, @LOOKUPR, @XLOOKUP, and @XLOOKUPR. See *Lookup Statements, External Lookup Statements,* and *Built-In Functions* for further information.

To create a derived column

1. Choose **R**eport from the Main Menu.

2. Choose **D**esign/Redesign a Report.

3. Type the name of the data file for which you are designing the report.

4. Press **Enter**.

5. Type a name for the report format and press **Enter**.

   Because you can use up to 31 characters in the name, you can be descriptive.

6. Select the records you want to print with the Retrieve Spec screen.

   To print all the records, press **F10**.

   For information on selecting records, see *Search/ Update* and *Search Options*.

7. When you see the Column/Sort Spec screen, type a number from 1 through 50 in the fields you want listed as columns. Add additional codes separated by commas to indicate how you want the data sorted and totalled. If you run out of room, press **F6** to expand the line.

   For a list of codes, see *Column/Sort Spec Codes*.

8. After you number the columns you want to print, make a note of the column numbers you will reference in your derived column figure.

   For instance, if you want to print a derived column that shows the result of SALES (Column 2) times COMMISSION RATE (Column 3), jot down these two column numbers.

9. Press **F8** to display the Derived Columns screen.

10. In the first Heading field, type the derived column's heading.

11. In the Formula field, type a formula that refers to the column numbers you used in the Column/Sort Spec screen.

    To multiply Column 2 by Column 3, for instance, you type

    #2*#3

12. In the Column Spec field, type the number of the column in which you want the derived figures to appear.

    Pick a number you have not used on the Column/ Sort Spec screen.

13. Repeat Steps 10 through 12 for additional derived fields.

14. Press **F10**.

15. Choose print options, if you want, and press **F10**.

16. Press **Y** to print the report or **N** to return to the Report Menu.

Design File

FILE

Purpose

Creates the form design (and a new database).

Notes

To create a Q&A database, you begin by choosing **D**esign File. This command enables you to specify where you want data fields to appear. You arrange the fields and type the labels, as if you were using a word processing program.

A Q&A form includes labels and fields. When you create the form, you lay out the labels using the tools available in Write. As you create the form, you can add lines or boxes using **D**raw In addition, and you assign information types to each field. The information type specifies what kind of data the user can type in the field. You also choose format options such as flush right alignment. Finally, if you chose numbers, money, hours, or date information types, you choose global format options for the display of this information.

In addition, you can center lines and create rectangular fields. A rectangular field is a multi-line field in which the second (turnover) lines are indented to align with the label. This alignment makes data entry easier and helps make the form easier to read. You can choose additional options by customizing the file (see *Customize a File*).

You cannot draw boxes around multi-line fields.

You can create a field that takes up an entire screen, and a form that occupies up to 10 screens in length.

The following function keys are available with the
Design File option:

Key	Function
F1	Provides Help.
Shift-F2	Macro Menu.
F3	Deletes block.
Ctrl-F3	Counts words, lines, and paragraphs.
F4	Deletes from cursor to end of field.
Shift-F4	Deletes all characters in field.
F5	Copies a block.
Shift-F5	Moves a block.
Ctrl-F5	Copies a block to a file.
Alt-F5	Moves a block to a file.
Alt-F6	Inserts a soft hyphen.
F7	Searches and replaces.
Shift-F7	Restores deletion.
Ctrl-F7	Displays Go To menu.
F8	Displays Options Menu.
Shift-F8	Sets Calc mode.
Ctrl-F8	Resets @NUMBER.
F10	Saves form design.

To access the design screen:

1. Choose File from the Main Menu.

2. Choose Design File.

To design a new file:

1. Choose File from the Main Menu.

2. Choose Design File.

3. Type the file name.

4. Choose Design a New File.

5. Press **F8** to see the Options screen so that you can draw lines or boxes or to set new tabs before you add fields.

   To set tabs, choose **S**et Tabs. See *Tabs* for more information. To add lines or boxes, choose **D**raw. See *Draw* for more information.

   Press **F10** when you finish with this option.

6. Place the cursor where you want a field to appear.

7. Type the field label followed by a colon (**:**).

   If you want to limit the field length to a number of characters you specify, insert the number of spaces you want by pressing the spacebar. Then type a greater-than symbol (**>**).

   To create a multi-line field, press **Enter** to leave blank lines. Then press **Tab** to move the cursor to the right edge of the form, and type a greater-than sign (**>**).

   If you plan to insert complex programming statements into a field, create a multiple-line field. You will have ample room to write the programming statement. For more information, see *Programming Statements*.

8. Press **Tab** or use the arrow keys to move to the next field's location.

9. Repeat Steps 6 through 10 until you enter all the fields.

10. Press **F10**.

11. Choose an Information Type and Format Options for each field, if you want.

    The default information type is **T**ext, and the default format spec is **J**ustify **L**eft.

12. Press **F10**.

    If you choose a **D**ate, **H**ours, **N**umber, or **M**oney information type, you see the Global Format Options screen. You can change the global formats for these fields, or press **F10** to continue.

To center a line

1. Place the cursor on the line you want to center.

2. Press **F8** to display the Options screen.

3. Choose **C**enter.

To create a rectangular multi-line field

1. When you finish typing the label, type a less-than symbol (**<**) instead of the colon.

2. Press **Enter** to leave blank lines.

3. Press **Tab** to place the cursor at the right edge of the form.

4 Type a greater-than symbol (**>**) to mark the end of the field.

Design/Redesign a Report

REPORT

Purpose

Creates or updates a report format.

Notes

In contrast to the Print command in the File Menu, which prints data record-by-record, the Report commands generate columnar output. Because Report has so many options, you must create a report format that records your print output choices.

When you use Design/Redesign a Report, you see the Column/Sort Spec screen, which looks exactly like the Retrieval Spec screen. You type codes in this screen's fields to determine which fields appear in columns and how Q&A should sort your output. For a list of codes, see *Column/Sort Spec Codes*.

If you type more than one code, be sure to separate the codes with commas. Here are some valid Column/Sort Spec codes and an explanation of what they do:

1, AS, AB   Sort the data in the field in ascending order (AS), and print this field in the first column (1). Break the column (AB) when the first letter changes.

3, ST, T   Print the data in this field in the third column (3), and print subtotals (ST) at every column break. Print totals at the bottom of the column (T).

Use the following function keys with the Column/Sort Spec screen:

Key	*Function*
F1	Provides Help.
Shift-F2	Displays Macro Menu.
F3	Deletes all specs.
F4	Deletes word.
Shift-F4	Deletes all characters in field.
Ctrl-F5	Enters current date.
Alt-F5	Enters current time.
F8	Displays Derived Columns screen.
F9	Returns to Retrieve Spec screen.
F10	Saves column/sort specs and continues.

To create a report format

1. Choose **R**eport from the Main Menu.

2. Choose **D**esign/Redesign a Report.

3. Type the name of the data file for which you are designing the report.

4. Press **Enter**.

5. Type a name for the report format and press **Enter**.

   You can use up to 31 characters in a name.

6. Select the records you want to print with the Retrieve Spec screen.

   To print all the records, press **F10**.

For information on selecting records, see *Search/Update* and *Search Options*.

7. When you see the Column/Sort Spec screen, type a number from 1 through 50 in the fields you want listed as columns. Add additional codes to indicate how you want the data sorted and totalled. Be sure to separate each code with a comma. If you run out of room, press **F6** to expand the line.

   For a list of codes, see *Column/Sort Spec Codes*.

   Press **F8** to create Derived Columns.

8. Press **F10**.

9. Choose print options.

   See *Print Options* for more information on this screen's options.

   To change the page definition for this report format only, press **F8** and choose new settings for margins, page size, characters per inch, headers, and footers from the Define Page screen. (For more information on these options, see *Define Page*. To change the page definition settings for all new report formats, see *Set Global Options*.)

10. Press **Y** to print the report or **N** to return to the Report Menu.

To redesign a report format

1. Choose **R**eport from the Main Menu.

2. Choose **D**esign/Redesign a report.

3. Type the name of the data file for which you are designing the report.

4. Press **Enter**.

5. Highlight the name of the report format and press **Enter**.

6. Select the records you want to print with the Retrieve Spec screen.

   To print all the records, press **F10**.

   For information on selecting records, see *Search/Update* and *Search Options*.

7. When you see the Column/Sort Spec screen, make the changes you want to make to the report format.

8. Press **F10**.

9. Choose print options, if you want, and press **F10**.

10. Press **Y** to print the report or **N** to return to the Report Menu.

Design/Redesign a Spec

FILE

Purpose

Formats database output for simple free-form or coordinate printing.

Notes

The Print command on the File Menu should be distinguished from the sophisticated Report capabilities; you use Print for producing simple output. Using this command, you can produce printed output quickly and easily. The Design/Redesign a Spec command enables you to specify which fields print, and in what order they print. You also can control where the fields appear on-screen.

Before creating a print spec, see *Set Global Options* for information on choosing print spec defaults. This command affects only *new* print specs, so make your choices before creating a print spec.

When you use the Design/Redesign a Spec command, you see the Print Spec screen. Q&A has the following styles of printing:

- Use Free Form codes for simple printouts that lack formatting such as headers and footers. You can specify which fields you want to print and in what order. You also can control spacing between fields and insert blank lines.

- Use Co-ordinate codes to specify exactly where on the page you want information to appear. Use this option to print to preprinted forms.

You cannot combine free-form codes and co-ordinate codes in a print spec; you must choose between them.

The free-form codes enable you to indicate which fields to print, and you can control the order in which they appear on the printout. You can add blank spaces, start new lines, and indicate the maximum number of characters to print from the field. A description on these codes follows:

- Use a number from 1 to 999 to indicate which fields you want printed and in what order they are to appear on the printout.

- After the number, press **x** (start a new line after printing the field) or **+** (skip a space after printing this field). To tell Q&A to skip additional spaces or lines after the field, enter a comma after the *x* or + and then type the number of additional spaces or lines you want skipped.

- Type a comma and a number indicating the maximum number of characters to print. Use this feature to make sure that an extra-long entry does not exceed the line length, which would cause printing problems.

The following are examples of correct free-form codes:

3x	Make this field the third to print, and start a new line after.
1+	First field, one blank space after.
1+,5	First field, five blank spaces after.
3x,2	Third field, two blank lines after.
5x,2,25	Fifth field, two blank lines after, 25 characters maximum.
5x,,25	Fifth field, 25 characters maximum (note that two commas are needed).

You can use Free Form reports for mailing labels, but it is easier to use the Mailing Label Menu in Write.

The co-ordinate codes enable you to specify where fields print on the page. This feature is useful for printing to preprinted business forms. If you type the coordinates

into a field, the field prints. (Blank fields do not print.)
Here's what you type, separated by commas:

- **Line Number** There are 66 lines on the page and 6
  lines to the inch. Line 6 is one inch from the top of
  the page.

- **Column Number** There are 85 character positions
  on a standard 8 1/2-wide page, assuming a standard
  Pica font.

- **Maximum Number of Characters** (optional) Type
  a number to indicate the maximum number
  characters to print.

The following codes are examples of correct form:

6,10   Begin field six lines from top, 10
                 spaces from left.

6, 25,25   Begin field six lines from top, 25
                 spaces from left, 25 characters
                 maximum.

See *Rename/Delete/Copy a Spec* for information on
renaming, deleting, or copying print specs.

To display the Print Spec screen

1. Choose **F**ile from the Main Menu.

2. Choose **P**rint.

3. Type the name of the database for which you want
   to design or redesign a print spec.

   You see a list of the Print Specs you created for this
   database. If you did not create any Print Specs, the
   screen is blank.

4. Type the Print Spec name and press **Enter**.

   If you create a new Print Spec, you can use up to 30
   characters; you needn't obey DOS conventions.

   You see the Retrieve Spec screen.

5. Retrieve the records you want to print.

   Press **F8** to sort the records.

If you want to print the entire database, press **F10** without specifying any search criteria to retrieve all the records.

See *Sort* for more information. See *Search/Update* for information on retrieving records.

After you retrieve the records, you see the Fields Spec screen.

6. Type the field specs to determine what information to print.

   To print all the fields on the form (as displayed on the form design), press **F10**.

   If you want to print some of the fields, choose between free-form and coordinate codes. Type the codes in the fields you want printed. Then press **F10**.

7. You can choose Print Options, if you want.

   You can press **F8** to choose page definition options for this print spec only. See *Define Page* for a list of these options, including headers and footers with page numbers, automatic date and time, and centered text. Press **F9** to return to the Print Options screen.

8. Press **F10**.

9. Press **Enter** to print the forms.

Ditto

FILE

Purpose

Copies data from a field in the previous form to the same field on a new, blank form. You also can copy all the data on a previously-viewed form to all the fields on a new, blank form.

Notes

Use this time-saving command when you enter the same information (such as a state or zip code) on forms.

You cannot use Ditto if you just pressed F9 or F10 to go back and forth between forms.

To copy information from a field on the immediately previous form

1. Place the cursor in the field to which you want to copy the information.

2. Press **F5**.

To copy the previously viewed form

1. Display the form using Search/Update.

2. Exit Search/Update and choose **A**dd data from the File Menu.

3. Press **Shift-F5**.

Draw

FILE, WRITE

Purpose

Adds lines or boxes to a form or document.

Notes

Even though you can display lines and boxes on your screen, your printer may not be able to print them. To find out whether your printer can print lines and boxes, create a new document, add a box, and try printing the document.

You can create single lines and double lines.

The lines and boxes you add are composed of ordinary, on-screen characters, which can be deleted or moved. After you create the line or box, be careful as you type to avoid disturbing these characters. Keep Insert mode off as you type so that Q&A does not push the lines or boxes aside to make room for the text you insert.

Use the following key characters to create lines and boxes:

Key	Draws line
Up arrow	Up
PgUp	Diagonally up and right
Right arrow	Right
PgDn	Diagonally down and right
Down arrow	Down
End	Diagonally down and left
Left arrow	Left
Home	Diagonally up and left

To add lines or boxes to a form or document

1. Place the cursor where you want the line or box to begin.

2. Press **F8** (Options).

3. Choose **D**raw.

4. Press one of the keys on the numeric keypad to begin drawing.

   Hold down the Shift key if you want to draw a double line. To lock double lines on, press **Num Lock**.

   To stop drawing and move the cursor to a new location, press **F6** to lift up the pen. Then press **F6** to lower the pen again.

   To erase a line, press **F8**. Then press **F8** to resume drawing.

5 Press **F10** when you finish drawing.

The following keys are the Draw function keys:

Key	*Function*
F6	Pen up/pen down.
F8	Erase.
F10	Exit Draw and resume editing.

Edit Header/Edit Footer

WRITE

Purpose

Creates a header for your document.

Notes

For information on creating headers or footers for database reports, see *Design/Redesign a Print Spec, Design/Redesign a Report Format,* and *Define Page* (FILE).

To suppress the printing of headers or footers on the first page of a document, see *Define Page* (WRITE).

To create a header or footer

1. Press **Ctrl-F8**.

2. Choose Edit **H**eader or Edit **F**ooter from the Options menu.

3. Type the header or footer text in the window.

   To include an automatic page number, type a pound sign (**#**).

   To include the current time, type **@TIME**(*n*), where *n* is one of the time codes (see *Date and Time Format Codes*).

   To include the current date, type **@DATE**(*n*), where *n* is one of the date codes (see *Date and Time Format Codes*).

4. Press **F10**.

Edit Lookup Table

FILE

Purpose

Creates or allows editing of the current data file's lookup table.

Notes

See *Lookup Statements* for an explanation of lookup tables and lookup statements.

The following keys are the Lookup Table function keys:

F1	Help
Shift-F2	Macros
F4	Delete cell entry
Ctrl-F4	Delete line
Ctrl-F5	Auto-type current date
Alt-F5	Auto-type current time
F6	Expand field for long programs
F10	Save and continue

To Create or Edit the Lookup Table

1. Choose **D**esign File from the File Menu.

2. Choose **C**ustomize File.

3. Type the name of the data file you want to customize.

   To see a list of available databases, press the spacebar to clear the line and press **Enter**.

4. Choose **E**dit Lookup Table.

   You see the Lookup Table screen for the current data file.

5. Type the key values in the Key column.

6. Type the corresponding values in column 1.

   If there isn't enough room to type values, press **F6**.

   To insert a line, position the cursor in the first space of the Key column and press **Enter**. To delete a line, press **Ctrl-F4**.

7. Type additional columns of corresponding values, if desired.

8. Press **F10** to save the table and continue.

Embedded Printing Commands

WRITE

Purpose

Enables you to change formats such as justification and line spacing as often as you want within a document. Also enables special features such as queued printing, date and time entry at time of printing, and printer pause.

Embedded Commands

Command	Meaning
*@DATE(*n*)*	Prints the date at the time of printing where *n* stands for one of the date format codes.
*@TIME(*n*)*	Prints the time at the time of printing where *n* stands for one of the time format codes.
*JOIN *filename**	Queues printing with continuous pagination, headers, and footers.
Justify No	Turns right-margin justification off.
Justify Yes	Turns right-margin justification on.
*LS*n**	Changes line spacing to *n* lines.
*PRINTER *code**	Embeds printer command.
*QUEUE *filename**	Queues printing.
*QUEUEP *filename**	Queues printing with continuous pagination.
STOP	Pauses printing at code's location in document so that you can change cartridges, etc. You press **Enter** to continue.

Export to ASCII

WRITE

Purpose

Exports a Write document to an ASCII-format file.

Notes

You can export Write documents to ASCII text in three ways:

- Choose the **S**tandard ASCII option to export your document with carriage returns at the end of each line.

- Choose the **D**ocument ASCII option to export your document with carriage returns at the end of each paragraph. The paragraphs must be separated by blank lines.

- Choose the **M**acintosh ASCII option if you intend to exchange the file with a Macintosh user.

To export a Write document with headers, footers, and pagination, *see* **Printing.**

To export to ASCII:

1. Choose **E**xport to ASCII.

2. Choose **S**tandard ASCII, **D**ocument ASCII, or **M**acintosh ASCII.

3. Type the ASCII file name and press **Enter**.

   The name must differ from the Write document's name.

External Lookup Statements

FILE

Purpose

Retrieves information from another Q&A database and inserts it into the current database.

Use XLOOKUP statements to retrieve information you stored in other Q&A databases. The external database must be in the same directory or disk as the current database (or otherwise accessible by Q&A), unless you type all the necessary path information when you name the external data file.

An external lookup statement is analogous to a Lookup Statement, but it retrieves values from an external database rather than the current database's lookup table.

Note the following terms:

- *Primary file* is the current database in which the retrieved information will appear.

- *Primary key field* is the field of the primary file in which the retrieved information will be displayed. The name of this field must match the name of the external key field.

- *External file* is the database from which the information will be retrieved

- *External key field is* a field of the external file that has exactly the same name as the primary key field.

- *Lookup field* is the field of the external file that contains the information to be retrieved.

You place the external lookup statement in a field of the primary file, such as the primary key field. The statement says, in effect, "Look in the external file named such-and-such, and find a record in which the external key field's contents match what's typed in the primary key field. Then go to the lookup field on the same record, copy the information in that field, and display it here."

Suppose that you type a company's code name (AMAL) in the primary key field. You write an external lookup statement that retrieves the full company name from a database of company names. The name of the primary key field is "Company Name Code." The name of the external key field is also "Company Name Code." The external lookup statement tells Q&A to search the company name database for the record that contains the company name code "AMAL." It finds the record. There is another field on this record called "Company Name—Full." This field is the lookup field. Q&A retrieves the information from the lookup field and displays it in the current record.

External lookup operations occur when you add or update a data record and press **F8** (Recalculate). See *Recalculation Mode*.

You must observe this syntax when you create the LOOKUP statement:

> **XLOOKUP**("*primary file name*"**,** *primary key field ID#***, "***external key field name***", "***lookup field name***",** *destination field ID#*)

Note that the ID numbers do not require quotation marks, but all file names and field names *do* require beginning and ending quotation marks.

Here's a valid XLOOKUP statement:

> **#90:XLOOKUP("CNAMES",#90, "Company Name Code","Company Name–Full",#90)**

Note that this statement appears in Field ID#90, employs this field as the primary key field, and places the retrieved information in this field. When you add data, the effect of such a statement is to replace the company code with the company full name when you press F8 or leave the record. You can use other fields as the primary key field and destination field if you want.

You must index the external key field before the external lookup function will work. For information on indexing fields, see *Speed Up Searches*.

An external lookup operation ignores uppercase and lowercase distinctions, but it returns the data with the capitalization pattern found in the external database.

Before you use an external lookup statement, make sure that your CONFIG.SYS file contains the statement FILES=20 (or a higher value). From the DOS prompt make the root directory current. Then type **TYPE CONFIG.SYS** and press **Enter**. If the CONFIG.SYS file does not contain a FILES statement, or if the number of files is less than 20, run the QAFILES program as directed below.

Q&A has two XLOOKUP statements:

- XLOOKUP returns the corresponding value *only when* an exact match is found. If no exact match is found, Q&A just leaves the field blank.

- LOOKUPR returns the corresponding value or, if no exact match is found, the next *lower* value that appears in the external database.

An XLOOKUP statement retrieves only one field at a time, but you can use additional XLOOKUP statements to retrieve additional fields from the external database. These four statements all use the same primary key field (#90), but they retrieve information from four different lookup fields and place the information in four different destination fields. Type the company code in field #90, press **F8**, and Q&A does the rest automatically.

#90:XLOOKUP("CNAMES",#90,
"Company Name Code",
"Company Name–Full",#90)

#91:XLOOKUP("CNAMES",#90,
"Company Name Code","Company
Address",#91)

#92:XLOOKUP("CNAMES",#90,
"Company Name Code","Company State",#92)

#93:XLOOKUP("CNAMES",#90,
"Company Name Code","Company Zip",#93)

If you want to use the retrieved value in a formula, use an external lookup function instead of a lookup statement. See @XLOOKUP and @XLOOKUPR in *Functions* for information on using the lookup functions.

See *Lookup Statements* for information on looking up information from the current database's lookup table.

To prepare the two databases

1. Design or redesign the files so that both have a field with the same name (such as "Company Name Code").

2. Use the Speed Up Searches option in the Customize Menu to index the external key field in the external file.

3. Add data to the external file.

   Make a list of the code names you use so that you will remember how to type the codes in the primary file.

4. Place both databases in Q&A's directory to simplify retrieval.

To create the XLOOKUP or XLOOKUPR statement

1. Choose **F**ile from the Main Menu.

2. Choose **D**esign File.

3. Type the name of the primary file.

4. Press **Enter**.

5. Choose **C**ustomize a File.

6. Press **Enter** to confirm the file name.

7. Choose **P**rogram File.

   You see the Program Spec screen.

8. Place the cursor in the field in which you want the external data value to appear.

9. Type a new field ID number (such as #110) followed by a colon.

10. Type **XLOOKUP** or **XLOOKUPR** and then type the following on one line, being careful to use exactly the punctuation that appears here. Press **F6** so you will have enough room.

    (*"external filename",primary field ID#,"external key field","lookup field "*, *destination field ID#*)

    Note that quotation marks are not required for field ID#s.

11. Press **F10** to save your XLOOKUP statement and return to the File menu.

To look up data in an external database automatically

1. Choose **A**dd Data or **S**earch/Update from the File Menu.

2. Type the name of the primary file.

To see a list of available databases, press the spacebar to clear the line and press **Enter**.

3. Place the cursor in the primary key field.

4. Type a key value or code that matches the key value or code you placed in the external key field of one of the records of the external file.

5 Press **F8**.

See *Recalculation Mode* for information on making recalculation automatic.

Field ID Number

FILE

Purpose

In form programming, assigns a unique number so the field can be referenced in formulas. You must assign a field ID# to each field you intend to mention in a Programming Statement.

Note

Bear in mind that Q&A executes the programming statements in order; Field #2 is executed before Field #5.

To assign an identification number to a field:

1. Choose **D**esign File from the File Menu.

2. Choose **C**ustomize a File from the Design Menu.

3. Type the name of the data file and press Enter.

4. Choose **P**rogram Form.

5. Place the cursor in the field to which you want to assign the identification number.

6. Type a pound sign followed by a whole number (integer).

The number should not appear as an ID number anywhere else on the form.

7. Press **F10** to save the ID numbers and continue.

See *Program Form* for information on writing
program statements.

Font Assignments

WRITE

Purpose

Assigns your printer's fonts to the Regular and Font
codes so that you can use them in your documents.

To install your printer's fonts

1. If you haven't already done so, install your printer.

   Choose Utilities from the Main Menu and Install a
   Printer from the Utilities Menu.

2. Choose Type/Edit from the Write Menu.

3. Press Ctrl-F9.

4. Place the cursor in the Font File Name field and
   press F6 to list the available files.

5. Use the arrow keys to select the correct font
   description file for your printer.

6. Move the cursor to the Regular field and press
   Enter to see a list of font options.

7. Use the spacebar or arrow keys to choose the font
   you want and press Enter.

8. Move the cursor to the next Font field and press
   Enter to see a list of font options.

9. Use the spacebar or arrow keys to choose the font
   you want and press Enter.

10. Repeat Steps 8 and 9 to assign up to 8 fonts.

11. Press F8 to make this Font Assignment Screen the
    default for all documents.

    If you don't press F8, the assignment is valid for the
    current document only.

12. Press F10.

Fonts

WRITE

Purpose

Enhances text so that it prints with one of your printer's fonts.

Note

To use fonts, you must install your printer and assign the fonts. See *Font Assignments* for more information.

To enhance text with fonts

1. Place the cursor at the beginning of the text you want to enhance.

   If you can't remember the number of the font you want, press **Ctrl-F9** to display the Font Assignments screen before proceeding.

2. Press **Shift-F6** to display the Enhancements menu.

3. Choose **F**ont.

4. Type the number of the font.

5. Use the arrow keys to select the text to enhance with the font you've chosen.

6. Press **F10**.

Format Options

FILE

Purpose

Specifies how text and values display and print. Assign the formats using the database's Format Spec screen.

Note

You can use more than one code in a field. For instance, the code **N,4,C,JR** formats a number with four decimal places, commas, and right-justified.

Formatting Options

Code	Application
JR	Aligns text, keyword, number, date, time, or Yes/No field flush right.
JC	Centers text, keyword, number, date, time, or Yes/No field.
JL	Aligns text, keyword, number, date, time, or Yes/No field flush left.
U	Displays text, keyword, or Yes/No field with uppercase letters.
0-7	Specifies number of decimal digits.
C	Inserts commas automatically in number and money fields.

Format Values

FILE

Purpose

Changes format options and information types to the database's format spec.

Notes

You choose alignments, decimal points, and other format options when you create the database in **D**esign File. You also can choose information types. If you want to change these items later, you can do so by choosing **F**ormat Values from the Customize Menu.

To change the format specs for a database

1. Choose **F**ile from the Main Menu.

2. Choose **D**esign File.

3. Type the name of the database you want to customize.

4. Press **Enter**.

5. Choose **C**ustomize a File.

6. Press **Enter** to confirm the file name.

7. Choose **F**ormat Values.

   You see the database's Format Spec.

8. Press **Tab** to select the field you want to change, and type new codes.

9. Press **F10** until you see your document again.

Functions

FILE

Purpose

Provides resources for constructing programming statements.

Notes

Use functions when you write programming statements to customize your file. For information on programming, see *Program File* and *Programming Statements*.

Q&A's Built-In Functions

@ABS(*n*)
A mathematical function that returns the absolute (positive) value of n.

@ADD
A context function that restricts execution of a programming statement to Add Data. The statement will not function in Search/Update.

@ASC(*"x"*)
A mathematical function that returns the ASCII decimal code of the first character of the string "x".

@AVG(*list*)
A mathematical function that computes the average of the fields referenced in the list.

@CGR(*pv, fv, np*)
A financial function that computes the rate of return on an investment (pv = present value; fv=future value; np=number of periods).

@CHR*(ASCII code)*
A text/string function that returns the ASCII character equivalent of an ASCII decimal code).

@D*(date)*
A date/time function that enables the use of a date as a constant in a programming statement.

@DATE
A date/time function that returns today's date.

@DEL(x,y,z)
A text/string function that returns x with z characters deleted starting at character y.

@DITTO*(list)*
A text/string function in Add Data that automatically copies the listed fields' values from the previous form to the new form.

@DOM*(n)*
A date/time function that returns an integer corresponding to the day of the date you typed in field n.

@DOW*(n)*
A date/time function that returns the name of the day you typed in field n.

@EXP*(x,y)*
A mathematical function that raises x to the y power.

@FILENAME
A text/string function that returns the name of the current data file.

@FV*(pa, i, np)*
A financial function that computes the future value of regular payments (pa=payment amount; i=interest; np=number of periods).

@HELP*(x)*
A text/string function that displays a custom help screen for the field x.

@INSTR*(x,y)*
A text/string function that returns an integer showing the position (counting left to right) of string y in the text x.

@INT*(n)*
A mathematical function that returns the integer (whole number) of n.

@LEFT(x,y)
A text/string function that returns the y leftmost characters of the string x.

@LEN(x)
A text/string function that returns the character length of the string in field x.

@LOOKUP(key, column)
A lookup function that returns the corresponding value from the current data file's lookup table if an exact match is found, and allows the value to be used in a programming statement. See *Lookup Statement* for an explanation of lookup tables and lookup procedures.

@LOOKUPR(key, column)
A lookup function that returns the corresponding value from the current data file's lookup table if an exact match is found. If an exact match is not found, returns the next lower value. Allows the value to be used in a programming statement. See *Lookup Statement* for an explanation of lookup tables and lookup procedures.

@MAX(list)
A mathematical function that returns the highest value in a list of referenced fields.

@MID(x,y,z)
A text/string function that returns z characters from the string x starting at position y.

@MIN(list)
A mathematical function that returns the lowest value in a list of referenced fields.

@MONTH$(n)
A date/time function that returns the name of the month you typed in field n.

@MONTH(n)
A date/time function that returns an integer corresponding to the month of the date you typed in field n .

@MSG(x)
A text/string function that displays the message x (maximum 80 characters) on the Message Line (bottom of screen).

@NUM*(x)*

A mathematical function that returns the number found in the referenced field x, even if the field also contains text.

@NUMBER

A numbering function that returns a unique number that is always one greater than the last @NUMBER that was automatically entered.

@NUMBER*(n)*

A numbering function that returns a unique number that is always n greater than the last @NUMBER(n) that was automatically entered.

@PMT*(pv,i,np)*

A financial function that computes the amount of the periodic payment due on a loan (pv=present value; i=interest rate per period; np=number of payments).

@PV*(pa,i,np)*

A financial function that computes the present value of an annuity (pa=amount of periodic payment; i=interest rate per period; np=number of payments).

@RIGHT*(x,y)*

A text/string function that returns the rightmost y characters of x.

@ROUND*(x,y)*

A mathematical function that rounds the value x to y decimal places.

@SGN*(x)*

A mathematical function that returns an integer showing whether the expression x is positive (+1), 0, or negative (-1).

@SQRT*(n)*

A mathematical function that returns the square root of n.

@STD*(list)*

A mathematical function that computes the standard deviation of a list of referenced fields.

@STR*(x)*

A text/string function that returns the text value of the number x.

@SUM*(list)*
A mathematical function that computes the sum of a list of referenced fields.

@T*(time)*
A date/time function that enables the use of a time as a constant in a programming statement.

@TEXT*(x,y)*
A text/string function that inserts y copies of the character or string x.

@TIME
A date/time function that returns the current time.

@UPDATE
A context function that restricts execution of a programming statement to Search/Update. The statement will not function in Add Data

@USERID
A multiuser function that inserts the current user's ID number in the field.

@VAR*(list)*
A mathematical function that computes the variance of a list of referenced fields.

@WIDTH*(x)*
A text/string function that returns an integer that indicates the width of the field x (in characters).

@XLOOKUP*(filename, primary key field, external key field, lookup field)*
A function that searches an external file and tries to match the value in the primary key field to a corresponding value in the external key field. If a match is found, returns the value in the lookup field.

@XLOOKUPR*(filename, primary key field, external key field, lookup field)*
A function that searches an external file and tries to match the value in the primary key field to a corresponding value in the external key field. If a match is found, returns the value in the lookup field. If no match is found, returns the next lower value.

@YEAR*(n)*
A date/time function that returns an integer corresponding to the year of the date you typed in field n.

Get

Purpose

Retrieves a document from disk.

Notes

After you retrieve a document with Get, it becomes the current document. Use Type/Edit to display it on-screen.

Q&A can read the following file formats directly: PFS:Write and IBM Writing Assistant. The program also enables you to import files created by WordStar, Lotus 1-2-3, and Symphony.

To retrieve a file from disk

1. Choose Get from the Write Menu.

2. Type the name of the document you want to retrieve.

4. Press Enter.

Global Format Options

Purpose

Changes global defaults for the display and printing of numbers, currency figures, times, and dates.

Notes

When you create a new database with Design File, you see the Global Format Options menu if you created fields with number, money, date, or hour information types.

For more information, see *Date and Time Display Codes.*

To change global format options (in Design File)

1. When you see the Global Format Options screen, highlight the option you want to change.

The default setting appears highlighted.

2. Press the left- or right-arrow keys to move the highlight to the option you want.

3. Press **F10** when you have finished selecting the options you want.

To change the global format options after you create the database design

1. Choose **F**ile from the Main Menu.

2. Choose **D**esign File.

3. Type the name of the database you want to customize.

4. Press **Enter**.

5. Choose **C**ustomize a File.

6. Press **Enter** to confirm the file name.

7. Choose **F**ormat Values.

8. Press **F10**.

9. When you see the Global Format Options screen, highlight the option you want to change.

The default setting appears highlighted.

10. Highlight the option you want.

11. Press **F10** when you finish selecting the options you want.

Go To

WRITE

Purpose

Moves the cursor to the specified page and line.

Notes

If you enter both a page number and line, the cursor moves to the beginning of the line. If you omit the line number, the cursor moves to the top of the page. If you omit the page number, the cursor moves to the line number you specify, counting from the first line of the document's first page.

To move to a line or page you specify

1. Press **Ctrl-F7**.

2. Enter a page number and a line number (optional).

   To mark your current location, press **F5**.

3. Press **F10**.

You can return to the original cursor location quickly by pressing **Ctrl-F7** and **Enter**.

Import Document

WRITE

Purpose

Assists the user in the retrieval of documents created with other word processing programs.

Notes

Q&A can read the following file formats directly: PFS:Write and IBM Writing Assistant.

If you try to retrieve a document with a file format other than the ones the program can read directly, you must assist the program by identifying the file format. You also can choose how you want an ASCII file displayed. These are the Import Document options:

- **A**SCII imports the document as a straight ASCII file, with carriage returns at the end of every line.

- **S**pecial ASCII imports the document as an ASCII file with carriage returns at the end of every paragraph (not every line).

- **W**ordStar imports a WordStar file. Q&A converts the file to the Q&A format.

- **L**otus 1-2-3 or Symphony imports a Lotus 1-2-3 or Symphony spreadsheet. For more information, see *Import Spreadsheet*.

To retrieve a non-Q&A document from disk

1. Choose **G**et from the Write Menu.

2. Type the name of the document you want to retrieve.

3. Press **Enter**.

4. When the Import Document Menu appears, choose **A**SCII, **S**pecial ASCII, or **W**ordStar.

Information Types

FILE

Purpose

Limits the type of information you can place in a field.

Notes

A field's information type determines what kind of information you can place in the blank. By default, Q&A assigns every field the Text information type. If you are entering numbers, keywords, dates, times, or yes/no information in a field, override the default information type. You will prevent the placement of the wrong kind of information in a field.

You can assign the information type when you create the form design. See *Design File*. You also assign information types after you create the form design, and even after you add data. See *Redesigning a File*.

Information Type Options

Code	Application
Text	Allows any character to be entered in the field.
Number	Limits input to numbers, commas, and decimal points.
Money	Formats numbers with dollar signs, commas, and two decimal places.
Keyword	Accepts keywords

Date	Accepts dates in three formats (June 20, 1990; 6/20/90; or 90-6-20) and reformats to the standard chosen in Global Formats.
Hours	Accepts hours in several formats (such as 4 PM, 4:00pm, or 4pm) and reformats to the standard chosen in Global Formats.
Yes/No	Accepts Yes, Y, True, T, or 1 for "yes," and No, N, False, F, or 0 for "no."

To change information types in an existing database design

1. Choose File from the Main Menu.
2. Choose Design File.
3. Choose Redesign a File.
4. Type the data file name.
5. Press F10.
6. Press Tab to select the field you want to change.
7. Type the new information type code.
8. Repeat Steps 6 and 7 for additional fields.
9. Press F10 until you see the File Menu.

Insert Document

WRITE

Purpose

Inserts an existing document into the current document.

Notes

This command inserts the imported document at the cursor's location. You can insert any Q&A document, as well as any imported document. See *Importing Lotus and Symphony Spreadsheets.*

You also can insert documents using the printer command *JOIN*. You don't see the inserted documents on-screen; they appear only in the printout. For more information, see *Embedded Printer Commands*.

To insert a document at the cursor's location
1. Press **F8** (Options).
2. Choose **I**nsert document.
3. Type the document name.
4. Press **Enter**.

Insert Mode

FILE, REPORT, ASSISTANT, WRITE

Purpose
Toggles the text entry/editing mode between the Overwrite and Insert modes.

Notes
Overwrite mode is the default for Q&A. The characters you type rub out existing text. In Insert mode, however, the text you type does not erase existing text.

To toggle the Insert/Overwrite modes:
Press **Ins**.

Justify Command

WRITE

Purpose
Turns right-margin justification on or off.

Notes
Justified text appears only on the printout. Place soft hyphens in lengthy words to avoid this unwanted effect.

You can justify the entire document by choosing Yes in the Justify option of the Print Options menu. To toggle justification on and off within a document, embed the *Justify Yes* and *Justify No* commands in the document. Use this command as many times as you want.

For a list of embedded commands, see *Embedded Printing Commands*.

To toggle justification on

1. In Type/Edit, place the cursor where you want the justification to begin.

2. Type *Justify Yes*.

   You can abbreviate the command to *JY Y*.

   To toggle justification off, type *Justify No*. You can abbreviate the command to *JY N*.

Keyword Reports

REPORT

Purpose

Creates a report format in which keywords are listed in the first column and all records that contain the keyword are grouped in additional columns.

Notes

You must design your database so that it includes at least one field employing the keyword information type (see *Design File* and *Information Types*). You must enter semicolons between each keyword. In addition, you must use the keywords consistently so that Q&A can group data by keyword.

To create a keyword report

1. Choose Report from the Main Menu.

2. Choose Design/Redesign a report.

3. Type the name of the data file for which you are designing the report.

4. Press **Enter**.

5. Type a name that contains up to 31 characters for the report format and press **Enter**.

6. Select the records you want to print with the Retrieve Spec screen.

   To print all the records, press **F10**.

7. When you see the Column/Sort Spec screen, type **1,K** in the keyword field.

8. Add additional codes to indicate which fields will print as additional columns.

   Separate each code with a comma. If you run out of room, press **F6** to expand the line.

9. Press **F10**.

10. Choose print options and press **F10**.

11. Press **Y** to print the report or **N** to return to the Report Menu.

Line Spacing

WRITE

Purpose

Sets line spacing.

Notes

To set the line spacing for the whole document, place the code at the beginning of the document. You can change line spacing within a document by placing the code on the line before you want the change to occur.

You also can choose single or double line spacing for the entire document using the Print Options (WRITE) menu.

For more information on embedded commands, see

Embedded Printing Commands.

To enter a line spacing code

1. Place the cursor on the line preceding the one on which you want the new line spacing to begin.

2. Type ***Ls** *n** where *n* is a whole number from 0 to 9.

Lookup Statements

FILE

Purpose

Retrieves information from the Lookup Table of the current database.

Notes

Use the LOOKUP statement to retrieve information from a lookup table that is stored with the database. You create the table by choosing the **E**dit Lookup Table command from the Customize Menu, and typing at least two columns of data: a column of key values and one or more columns of corresponding values. Q&A finds the corresponding value by checking the value in a field you specify (called the Key field), and attempting to match the value in the key value column. If a match is found, Q&A returns the value it finds in the corresponding value column and displays this value on the screen.

Q&A has the following LOOKUP statements:

- **LOOKUP** returns the corresponding value *only* when an exact match is found. If no exact match is found, Q&A just leaves the field blank.

- **LOOKUPR** returns the corresponding value or, if no exact match is found, the next *lower* value.

Suppose that a college instructor customizes a data file with a lookup table that translates numerical grades into letter grades. A student's cumulative, weighted average for the course is 3.835. The instructor creates a LOOKUPR statement that says, in effect, "Consult the Lookup Table to find the letter grade equivalent of this numerical grade. Then display the letter grade in this field." Here's what the lookup table looks like:

KEY	1
2	3
4	
4	A
3.825	A-
3.5	B+
3.375	B
2.825	B-
2.5	C+
2.375	C
1.825	C-
0.825	D
0	F

Q&A attempts to match the key value to a value in the KEY column. It fails to find a match, so the program uses the next lower value (3.825), which corresponds to an A-.

Use the following syntax when you type lookup statements:

LOOKUP(*key, column, field ID#*)

- *Key* refers to the ID number of the field that contains the value to look up.

- *Column* refers to the number of the column containing the corresponding value, the one you want displayed instead of the key value.

- *Field ID#* refers to the field in which you want the corresponding value displayed.

You can type up to four columns of corresponding values, but Q&A retrieves only one corresponding value at a time.

You can mix information types in a lookup table, and the table can contain up to 64,000 characters of information.

If you want to use the corresponding value in the formula, use a lookup function instead of a lookup statement.

See *External Lookup* for information on looking up information from other Q&A databases.

To Create a Lookup Table

1. Choose **D**esign File from the File Menu.

2. Choose **C**ustomize File.

3. Type the name of the data file you want to customize.

4. Choose **E**dit Lookup Table.

   You see the Lookup Table screen for the current data file.

5. Type the key values in the Key column.

6. Type the corresponding values in column 1.

   If there isn't enough room to type values, press **F6**.

   To insert a line, position the cursor in the first space of the Key column and press **Enter**. To delete a line, press **Ctrl-F4**.

7. Type additional columns of corresponding values.

8. Press **F10** to save the table and continue.

To create a LOOKUP or LOOKUPR statement

1. Choose **F**ile from the Main Menu.

2. Choose **D**esign File.

3. Type the name of the database you want to customize.

4. Press **Enter**.

5. Choose **C**ustomize a File.

6. Press **Enter** to confirm the file name.

7. Choose **P**rogram File.

8. Place the cursor in the field in which you want the corresponding value to appear.

9. Type a new field ID number (such as #110) followed by a colon.

10. Type **LOOKUP** or **LOOKUPR**, and in parentheses, indicate the field ID# of the field from which the lookup value is to be drawn, the column from which the corresponding value is to be

retrieved, and the field ID# of the field in which you want the retrieved value to be displayed, as in the following example:

LOOKUP(#9,1,#110)

Press **F6** to expand the field.

11. Press **F10** to save your lookup statement.

Macros

FILE, REPORT, WRITE

Purpose

Combines a sequence of functions into one command.

To define a macro

1. Press **Shift-F2**.

2. Choose **D**efine Macro.

3. Press a key to identify the macro.

   Press any character, function key, or key combination using Shift, Alt, or Ctrl. Use Alt-key combinations with letters from the keyboard, such as Alt-A, and Alt-B.

4. Record the macro by actually carrying out the action you want the macro to perform.

5. Press **Shift-F2** to turn off the macro recorder.

6. To save the macro to disk, press **Enter**. To retain the macro in memory, press **Esc**.

   You can redefine a macro by following the steps you used to define a macro.

To save the macros in memory

1. Press **Shift-F2**.

2. Choose **S**ave macros.

3. Type the file name.

   To save macros to a generic macro file press **Enter**. To save to a different file, type the file name.

To play back a macro

Press the key you used to identify the macro.

To retrieve a macro file

1. Press **Shift-F2**.

2. Choose **G**et Macros.

3. Type the name of the macro file.

   To see a list of the macro files, press the spacebar and press **Enter**. Choose the macro file name you want and press **Enter**.

4. Press **Enter**.

To clear a macro file from memory

1. Press **Shift-F2**.

2. Choose **C**lear Macros.

Mail Merge

FILE, WRITE

Purpose

Generates personalized form letters by drawing data from a File database and inserting it into a Write document.

Notes

After you create the merge document, you print the merge document with Write.

You can print the entire database, or use all of File's retrieval capabilities to retrieve just the records you want to print. You also can sort the records before printing, if you want. Write automatically draws data from the File database to complete the letter, printing one copy for each record in the database.

When Q&A extracts information from your database, the inserted text takes up only as much room as is needed.

To create a merge document

1. Type the text of the letter, but omit the specifics (such as name and address).

2. Place the cursor where you want the field code inserted and press **Alt-F7**.

3. Type the name of the database.

4. Highlight the field names you want to insert.

   To scroll through the list of field names, press **PgUp**, **PgDn**, **Home**, **End**, or the arrow keys.

5. Press **Enter**.

6. Repeat Steps 2 through 5 to add all the field codes you want to use.

   You can add (L)eft or (R)ight codes to control the spacing of the inserted data. Type the code before the closing asterisk.

7. Press **Shift-F8** to save your document.

To print a merge document

1. Display the merge document and press **F2**.

2. Press **Tab** to choose the Name Merge File field, and type the name of the database you are using.

3. Use the Retrieve Spec screen to retrieve just the documents you want to print.

   To print all the records, press **F10** .

   To sort the records before printing, press **F8**.

Mailing Labels

FILE, WRITE

Purpose

Generates mailing labels by drawing data from a File database and inserting it into a Write document.

Notes

Q&A is designed to use commercial mailing labels from firms such as Avery, Moore, and others.

You can print the entire database, or use all of File's retrieval capabilities to retrieve just the records you want to print.

To create mailing labels

1. Choose Mailing Labels from the Write Menu.

2. Select the name or size of mailing labels you use.

3. Press F10.

   You see an on-screen simulation of the mailing label, with the field codes *First name*, *Last name*, *Address*, *City*, *State*, and *Zip* already inserted.

   To add additional codes, press Alt-F7 and type the name of the database. To see a list of available databases, press the spacebar to clear the line and press Enter. Highlight the name of the database you want to use. Highlight the name of the field names you want to insert. Then press Enter. Repeat these steps to add additional codes.

4. Press Shift-F8 to save your document.

To print mailing labels

1. Display the mailing label document and press F2.

2. Press Tab to select the name of the merge file field, and type the name of the File database.

   Try printing with the default settings, and if you see problems, display this screen again and make the necessary changes.

3. Press F10.

4. Use the Retrieve Spec screen to retrieve just the documents you want to print.

   To print all the records, press F10.

   To sort the records before printing, press F8.

Mass Update

FILE

Purpose

Makes changes to two or more forms at once.

Notes

The Mass Update command performs this operation automatically, although you can confirm each update before it is made.

To perform a mass update

1. Choose **M**ass Update from the File Menu.

2. Type the name of the database you want to update.

3 Press **Enter**.

   You see a Retrieve Spec screen.

4. Retrieve the records you want to update.

   Press **F10** to retrieve all the records.

   After you retrieve the records, you see the Update Spec screen.

5. Press **Tab** to reach the field you want to update.

6. Type a pound sign (**#**) and a unique number, followed by an equals sign.

   Because this number differs from the Field ID numbers you assigned if you programmed the form, you can duplicate those numbers.

7. Type the change.

   You can type text, a formula, or a conditional expression.

   The following formula increases the value in a field by 15 percent:

   #1=#1* 1.15

   This formula changes the text in a field:

   #1="Acme International"

   Enclose text in quotation marks.

8. Press **F10** to begin the update.

9. Press **Enter** to preview each confirmation before it is made; type **N** and press **Enter** to update all the forms without confirmation.

   If you are confirming the updates, press **Shift-F10** to confirm the update or **F10** to see the next record without updating.

Newpage

WRITE

Purpose

Inserts a page break at the cursor location.

To force a new page

1. Place the cursor where you want the page break to occur.

2. Press **F8** (Options).

3. Choose **N**ewpage.

To delete a page break

1. Place the cursor on the page break symbol.

2. Press **Del**.

Operators

FILE

Purpose

Provides the symbols needed to express arithmetic, relational, and logical statements in form programs.

Note

Q&A evaluates expressions according to rules of precedence (rather than left to right). You can override the precedence rules using parentheses. See *Program the Form* and *Programming Statements*.

List of Operators

Operator	Purpose
+	Addition
-	Subtraction
*	Multiplication
/	Division
=	Equal to
<	Less than
>	Greater than
<=	Less than or equal to
=>	Greater than or equal to
<>	Not equal to
AND	Both comparisons true
OR	Either comparison true
NOT	Reverses comparisons' values

Order of Precedence

Operator	Precedence
division, multiplication	first
addition, subtraction	second
relational (< > <= => <>)	third
logical (NOT)	fourth
logical (AND, OR)	last

Print

FILE

Purpose

Produces printed output quickly and simply.

Notes

The Print command in the File Menu lacks many of Report's sophisticated features, such as the capacity to sort records, print data in columns, perform calculations, and look up information in other Q&A databases.

For more information, see *Design/Redesign a Spec* and *Print Forms.* To reset the default printing options, see *Set Global Options.*

Print a Document

WRITE

Purpose

Prints Write documents, including envelopes, merge documents, and mailing labels.

To print a document

1. If the document is not current, choose **G**et from the Write Menu to display it.

2. Press **F2**.

3. Choose print options, if you want.

4. Press **F10** to begin printing.

Print Forms

FILE

Purpose

Prints simple free-form printouts, coordinate printouts, and copies of forms as they appear on-screen.

Notes

For more complex printouts, see *Report*.

If you want to choose which fields to print, see *Design/ Redesign a Spec*.

To print forms while adding or updating data, see *Single Form Printing*.

To print all the records in the database, one to a page

1. Choose **P**rint from the File Menu.

2. Choose **P**rint Forms.

3. Press **F8** to sort the records.

   For information on sorting, see *Sort*.

4. Press **F10** without choosing a print spec or typing a print spec's name.

5. Press **F10** to select all the records.

6. Press **F10** to select all the fields.

7. Choose Print Options, if you want.

   By default, Q&A does not print the field labels. To print the field labels, tab to Print Field Labels and choose **Y**es.

8. Press **F10** to start printing.

To print using a print spec you created

1. Choose **P**rint from the File Menu.

2. Choose **P**rint Forms.

3. Use the arrow keys to choose a print spec or type the print spec's name.

4. Press **F10**.

5. Press **Y** to make temporary changes to the print spec, if you want, or press **Enter** to continue.

Print Options

FILE, REPORT

Purpose

Displays your options for printing database output.

Notes

You can choose to route output to up to five different printers, as well as print to disk or the screen. You can choose manual or continuous paper feed, the bin from which paper is drawn (for multibin printers); choose to offset the page by the number of characters you specify; send printer control codes to the printer; include or omit field labels; print more than one copy; print more than one form per page; and print more than one label across the page.

To choose print options

1. Press **Tab** to see the options.

2. Press the spacebar to highlight the option you want or type a new value.

3. Repeat Steps 1 and 2 for additional fields.

4. Press **F10** to start printing.

Print Options Function Keys

Key	Function
F1	Info
F8	Go to Define Page screen
F10	Save changes and print

Keys for Scrolling Reports

Key	Scrolls
Down arrow	Down one line
End	Right edge of report
Enter	Next screen
F10	Next screen

Home	Left edge of report
Left arrow	Previous column
PgDn	Next screen
PgUp	Previous screen
Right arrow	Next column
Up arrow	Up one line

Print Options

WRITE

Purpose

Displays options for printing Write documents.

Notes

You can choose the following options in this menu:

- **From page** specifies the page on which printing starts.

- **To page** specifies the page on which printing stops.

- Number of copies specifies the number of copies you want printed.

- **Print offset** establishes the position from which the print head starts printing.

- **Line spacing** sets single space or double space for the entire document. You also can choose a special envelope setting. To change line spacing more than once within a document, see *Line Spacing*.

- **Justify** enables you to choose whether your document is justified. If you choose justification, Write attempts to even the right margin by adding spaces between the words on a line.

- **Print to** sets up more than one printer or sets up a single printer with multiple modes. You also can print a fully formatted version of your document (complete with page numbers, headers, and pagination) to disk in ASCII format.

- **Type of paper feed** sets continuous or manual printing.

- **Number of columns** enables you to print up to eight columns on-screen. You don't see the columns until the document prints, and you can't change column spacing within the document. To change the spacing between columns (.25" by default), see *Set Global Options* (WRITE).

- **Printer control codes** turns special features on or off, such as condensed printing.

- **Name of Merge File**. For more information on this option, see *Mail Merge*.

The choices you make affect the current document. To change the default Print Options for all documents you create with Write, see *Set Global Options*.

To choose print options

1. Press **Tab** to display the option you want to change.

2. Highlight the option you want or type a new value.

3. Repeat Steps 1 and 2 for additional fields.

4. Press **F10** to start printing.

Print Options Function Keys

Key	Function
F1	Provides Help.
Ctrl-F6	Displays Design Page screen.
F9	Saves changes and goes back without printing.
F10	Saves changes and prints.

Print Queuing

WRITE

Purpose

Organizes print jobs into one file that you can print at one time.

To print a series of documents without continuous pagination

1. Choose **C**lear from the Write Menu.

2. Choose **T**ype/Edit.

3. Embed the following commands in this blank document:

   *QUEUE *document 1**
   *QUEUE *document 2**
   *QUEUE *document 3**

   document 1 is the DOS file name of the first document you want to print, *document 2* is the file name of the second, and *document 3* is the third.

To print a series of documents with continuous pagination

1. Choose **C**lear from the Write Menu.

2. Choose **T**ype/Edit.

3. Embed the following commands in this blank document:

   *QUEUEP *document 1**
   *QUEUEP *document 2**
   *QUEUEP *document 3**

   document 1 is the DOS file name of the first document you want to print, *document 2* is the file name of the second, and *document 3* is the third,.

To print a series of documents with continuous pagination, headers, and footers

1. Use the **G**et command in the Write Menu to load the first document.

2. Add headers and footers and page numbering.

3. Place the cursor at the end of the document.

4. Type the following:

   *JOIN *document name**

   document name is the DOS file name of the document to be placed at the cursor's location.

5. Repeat Steps 3 and 4 to join additional documents.

6. Press **F2** (Print) and proceed with printing.

Printer Codes

WRITE

Purpose

Enables control within a Write document of printer special effects, such as condensed mode printing, expanded mode printing, shadow mode printing, or near-letter quality mode printing.

Notes

To embed printer control codes in the text, you type a Write embedded command (for more information on embedded commands, see *Embedded Printer Commands*). This command includes the decimal ASCII equivalent of the printer's special effects command code. To find out what these codes are, see your printer's manual.

To embed printer control codes in the document

1. Place the cursor where you want the special effect to begin.

2. Type the following:

   *PRINTER *code1*, *code2*, *code3**

   where *code 1* refers to the first ASCII decimal equivalent of the control code used to turn on special effects, *code2* refers to the second, and *code3* to the third.

3. Move the cursor where you want the special effect to end.

4. Type the following:

   *PRINTER *code1*, *code2*, *code3**

   where *code 1* refers to the first ASCII decimal equivalent of the control code used to turn off special effects, *code2* refers to the second, and *code3* to the third.

Printing Envelopes

WRITE

Purpose

Finds the correspondent's address in a letter and prints the address on an envelope.

Notes

You must type the address using the correct format (see Step 1 below). Write prints the address beginning eight lines down from the top of the envelope and indents 3 1/2 inches.

To print an envelope

1. Type the letter using centered text for the address. The first flush left line should be the date. Leave a blank line after the date and type the correspondent's address flush left. Leave a blank line after the correspondent's address.

2. Insert an envelope in the printer. Line up the top of the envelope with the print head.

3. Press **F2**.

4. Choose the Line Spacing option by pressing the **down-arrow** key.

5. Choose **E**nvelope.

6. Press **F10**.

Program Form

FILE

Purpose

Displays the Program Spec screen so that you can create programming statements.

Notes

See *Programming Statements* for more information.

To access the program spec screen

1. Choose **F**ile from the Main Menu.

2. Choose **D**esign File.

3. Type the name of the database you want to customize, press the spacebar to clear the line and press **Enter**.

4. Press **Enter**.

5. Choose **C**ustomize a File.

6. Press **Enter** to confirm the file name.

7. Choose **P**rogram File.

Program Spec Function Keys

Key	Function
F1	Displays how to program.
Shift-F2	Macros.
F3	Clears current spec.
F4	Deletes from cursor to end of field.
Shift-F4	Deletes all characters in field.
Ctrl-F5	Enters current date.
Alt-F5	Enters current time.
F6	Expands field for long programs.
F7	Goes to Search/Update and displays Retrieve Spec Screen.
F10	Saves and continues.

Programming Statements

FILE

Purpose

Embeds instructions in fields that perform calculations, guides the cursor, looks up values in lookup tables or other File databases, or executes if a condition is met.

Notes

You can use programming statements to accomplish the following:

- Perform a calculation using values drawn from other fields.

- Look up values in the current database's Lookup Table.

- Look up values in another, separate Q&A database.

- Move the cursor around the screen after the user finishes typing in a field.

- Instruct Q&A to execute an instruction only if a condition is met. See *Conditional Statements.*

- Create complex statements that combine two or more of the above.

In manual recalculation mode (the default), programming statements are executed only when you press **F8** (Calculate). Press **Shift-F8** to choose automatic recalculation, in which all statements are executed every time the cursor leaves a field that has just been altered. See *Recalculation Mode.*

You may include instructions in programming statements so that they automatically execute upon movinginto the field or out of the field. You may also instruct Q&A to perform calculations on a given field upon entering or on leaving the record.

Apart from fields you have specified as entry or exit calculation fields, Q&A calculates fields in the order you number them when you assign field ID numbers.

If you run out of room while typing the formula, press **F6**. You can type up to 240 characters after you expand the field, with a maximum of 20,000 expanded field characters per database.

To create a programming statement

1. Choose **F**ile from the Main Menu.

2. Choose **D**esign File.

3. Type the name of the database you want to customize.

4. Press **Enter**.

5. Choose **C**ustomize a File.

6. Press **Enter** to confirm the file name.

7. Choose **P**rogram File.

8. Type field ID numbers in all fields to be referenced by a programming statement.

9. Type the programming statement in the field.

If you want Q&A to execute the statement when you move the cursor into the field, begin the statement with a less-than sign (<). If you want Q&A to execute the statement when you move the cursor out of the field, begin the statement with a greater-than sign (>).

If the statement that follows is a formula that returns a value that you want in the field, type an equal sign followed by the rest of the statement. If the statement that follows is a lookup statement, an external lookup statement, a cursor movement statement, or a conditional statement, type a colon.

You can combine two or more programming statements by linking them with semicolons.

10. Repeat Steps 8 and 9 to write additional programming statements.

11. To execute a statement upon entering or leaving the record, press **F8**. Then type the entry field ID # and the exit field ID# and press **Enter**.

12. Press **F10** to save your programming statements and return to the File Menu.

Recalculation Mode

FILE

Purpose

Controls the way Q&A performs calculations or executes programming statements.

Notes

By default, Q&A performs calculations only when you press **F8**. If you have used programming statements in your form, calculations may not be correct if you forgot to press F8. For this reason, change the default recalculation mode to automatic calculation. In automatic calculation, the form is recalculated every time the cursor leaves a field in which you have embedded a programming statement.

To change the default calculation mode

1. In Search/Update or Add Data, press **Shift-F8**.

2. Choose **A**utomatic Calc or **M**anual Calc.

Redesign a File

FILE

Purpose

Enables you to make changes to the database design even after data has been entered.

Notes

Be careful not to alter the field tags, the internal codes (such as AA, AB, or AC) that appear on the design screen. If you accidentally delete one of the field tag characters, type it back exactly the way it appeared. If you move a field, be sure to move the field tags too.

To redesign a database

1. Choose **F**ile from the Main Menu.

2. Choose **R**edesign a File.

3. Type the name of the database you want to redesign.

4 Press **Enter** to confirm the file name.

   When the design screen appears, you can change a label, lengthen or shorten an information blank, move a field, add a field, or delete a field.

5. Press **F10** to save the changes.

If you see an error message, you shortened or deleted a field. Make sure that the changes will not truncate or lose valuable data. If you want to continue, press **F10**. Otherwise, press **Esc**.

6. Change the Information Type or Format Spec of any field, if you wish, and define information types for new fields (if you added any).

7. Press **F10**.

   If your form has number, money, date, or time fields, you see the Global Format Options screen. Make changes, if you want.

8. Press **F10**.

To redesign the file

1. Press **F8** to draw lines or boxes or to set new tabs before you add fields.

   To set tabs, choose **S**et Tabs. To add lines or boxes, choose **D**raw.

2. Place the cursor where you want a field to appear.

3. Type the field label followed by a colon (**:**).

   If you want to limit the field length, insert the number of spaces you want by pressing the spacebar. Then type a greater-than symbol (**>**).

   To create a multi-line field, press **Enter** to leave blank lines. Then press **Tab** to move the cursor to the right edge of the form, and type a greater-than sign (**>**).

4. Press **Tab** or use the arrow keys to move to the next field's location.

5. Repeat Steps 2 through 4 until you enter all the fields.

6. Press **F10**.

7. Choose an Information Type and Format Options for each field, if you want.

   The default information type is **T**ext, and the default format spec is **J**ustify **L**eft.

8. Press **F10**.

If you choose a **D**ate, **H**ours, **N**umber, or **M**oney information type, you see the Global Format Options screen. Change the global formats for these fields, if you want, or press **F10** to continue.

To change a label

1. Place the cursor on the label you want to change.

2. Press **Backspace**, **Del**, **F4**, or **Shift-F4** to delete text. Press **Ins** to insert text within the label.

To change a field length

1. Place the cursor within the information blank.

2. Press the spacebar to add space, or press **Del** to remove space. Type a greater-than sign (**>**) to show where you want the field to end.

To move a field

1. Place the cursor on the first character of the field's label.

2. Press **Shift-F5**.

3. Highlight the label and the codes.

4. Press **F10**.

5. Move the cursor to the place where you want the field to appear.

6. Press **F10**.

To add a field

1. Press **Ins**.

2. Place the cursor where you want the new field to appear.

3. Type the field label, followed by a colon.

You may use the less-than symbol (<) to define a rectangular multiline field, or use the greater-than symbol (>) to show where you want the field to end.

To delete a field

Remove the field label and the field tag (codes such as AB or AC).

To change the information type

1. Perform editing tasks such as changing labels or moving fields.

2. Press **F10** to display the Format Spec screen.

3. Type the new information type code. You can change the format spec for each field.

   For lists, *see* Information Types.and Format Options.

4. Press **F10** until you see the File Menu.

Remove

FILE

Purpose

Deletes a group of data records from the database.

Notes

Note that once you remove records you cannot retrieve them. You see a Warning screen when you attempt to carry out a Remove operation. It might be wiser to make a copy of the database and remove the unwanted records from the copy.

To remove records from the database

1. Choose **R**emove from the File Menu.

2. Type the name of the database you want to customize.

3. Press **Enter**.

4. Type the search criteria.

   Remember that you want to retrieve the records you want to delete, not the ones you want to keep!

5. Press **F10** to retrieve the records.

6. Press **Y** to confirm the deletion or **N** to cancel.

Rename a Document

WRITE

Purpose

Renames a Write document.

To rename a Write document

1. Choose **R**ename a document from the Write Utilities menu.

2. Type the name of the file you want to rename.

3. Press **Enter**.

4. Type the new name.

5. Press **Enter**.

Rename/Delete/Copy a Spec

FILE

Purpose

Provides housekeeping functions for print specs.

Note

Use this command to give a print spec a more descriptive name, delete unwanted print specs, or use an existing print spec as the basis for a new one.

To change the name of a print spec

1. Choose **P**rint from the File Menu.

2. Type the name of the database that contains the print spec.

3. Press **Enter**.

4. Choose **R**ename/Delete/Copy a spec.

5. Choose **R**ename a print spec.

6. Type the print spec's present name and press **Enter**.

   If you cannot remember the name, press **Enter** to see a list. Then press **F10** to continue.

7. Type the new name and press **Enter**.

To delete a print spec

1. Choose **P**rint from the File Menu.

2. Type the name of the database that contains the print spec.

3. Press **Enter**.

4. Choose **R**ename/Delete/Copy a spec.

5. Choose **D**elete a print spec.

6. Type the print spec's present name and press **Enter**.

7. Press **Y** to confirm the deletion.

To use an existing print spec as the basis for another

1. Choose **P**rint from the File Menu.

2. Type the name of the database that contains the print spec.

3. Press **Enter**.

4. Choose **R**ename/Delete/Copy a spec.

5. Choose **C**opy a print spec.

6. When you see `Copy From`, type the print spec's name and press **Enter**.

7. Type the name of the new print spec and press **Enter**.

Restrict Values

FILE

Purpose

Customizes the database by restricting the range of values that can be typed into a field.

Notes

Use this feature to make sure that the user types a value into an important field, and to make sure that numeric values are typed within a permissible range. You can also define a list of valid responses; if the user types anything else, a warning message appears.

To access the Customize Menu

1. Choose File from the Main Menu.

2. Choose Design File.

3. Type the name of the database you want to customize.

4. Press Enter.

5. Choose Customize a File.

6. Press Enter to confirm the file name.

To restrict values

1. Choose Restrict Values from the Customize Menu.

2. Position the cursor on the field you want to restrict.

3. Type the value restriction symbol.

4. Type value restriction symbols in additional fields, if you want.

5. Press F10.

Value Restriction Options

Symbol	Function
x	Equal to x. Finds exact match only
=x	Equal to x. Finds exact match only.
/x	Finds everything except x.
/=	Finds any field with data.
x;y	Finds x or y.
>x	Finds greater than x. You cannot use this symbol in Yes/No fields.
<x	Finds less than x.
>=x	Finds greater than or equal to x. You cannot use this symbol in Yes/No fields.

<=x	Finds less than or equal to x. You cannot use this symbol in Yes/No fields.
x..y	Begins with x and ends with y.
>x..<y	Finds greater than x and less than y. You cannot use this symbol in Yes/No fields.
?	Used as wildcard for any character. Use this symbol for text and keyword fields only.
..	Finds any number of characters. Use this symbol for text and keyword fields only.
x..	Finds entry that begins with x. Use this symbol for text and keyword fields only.
..x	Finds entry that ends with x. Use this symbol for text and keyword fields only.
x..y	Entry must begin with x and end with y. Use this symbol for text and keyword fields only.
..x..	Entry must include x. Use this symbol for text and keyword fields only.
..x..y..z..	Entry must include x, y, and z in that order. Use this symbol for text and keyword fields only.

Restrict Spec Function Keys

Key	*Function*
F1	Displays how to restrict values.
F6	Expands the field to make room for more symbols.
F10	Saves restrictions and continues.

Save

WRITE

Purpose

Saves the current document to disk.

To save your document

1. In Type/Edit, press **Shift-F8**. Alternatively, choose **S**ave from the Write Menu.

2. Type the name of the file.

   If you previously saved the file, you see the file name on-screen.

3. Press **Enter**.

Search and Replace

WRITE

Purpose

Finds (and optionally replaces) a word or phrase in a Write document.

Notes

You can perform a simple or advanced search. In a simple search, Write finds the search phrase and, if you want, replaces it with another one. In an advanced search, you can choose additional search specifications such as case and search direction (backward and forward). In addition, you can use wild-card characters, search for formats (such as text enhancements and fonts), and perform sophisticated pattern-matching searches.

Wild-card characters

Character	Meaning
?	Any single character.
..	Any number of characters.

9   Any single number.

a   Any single alphabetical character.
               To use this character, choose Pattern
               in the Type option of the Search
               menu.

~   Any single non-alphanumeric
               character. To use this character,
               choose Pattern in the Type option of
               the Search menu.

Format codes

Code	Format
@BD	Boldface text enhancement
@CR	Carriage return
@CT	Centered line
@F1	Font 1
@F2	Font 2
@F3	Font 3
@F4	Font 4
@F5	Font 5
@F6	Font 6
@F7	Font 7
@F8	Font 8
@IT	Italic text enhancement
@NP	Hard page break (new page)
@RG	Regular text
@SB	Subscript text enhancement
@SP	Superscript text enhancement
@UL	Underline text enhancement
@XO	Strikeout text enhancement

To perform a simple search

1. Press **F7**.

2. Type the search phrase.

   You may use the ? and .. wildcards. You also may search for formats using the @ codes.

3. Press **F10**.

4. If a match is found, press **F7** to look for the next occurrence of the search phrase, edit the text, or press **Esc** to cancel the search.

   If no match is found, you see a message and the search is cancelled.

To repeat the last search

Press **F7** and **F10** to repeat the last search.

To perform a simple search and replace

1. Press **F7**.

2. Type the search phrase.

3. Press **Enter** or **Tab**.

4. Type the replacement text.

5. Press **F10**.

6. If a match is found, press **F10** to make the replacement. Press **F7** to look for the next occurrence. Press **Esc** to cancel the search.

   If no match is found, you see a message and the search and replace operation is cancelled.

To perform a case-sensitive search or search and replace

1. Press **F7**.

2. Press **PgDn** to display the advanced features.

3. Use the **Tab** key to select the Case option, and press the spacebar to choose Sensitive.

4. Use the **Tab** key to select the Search for: option, and type the search phrase.

   Be sure to type the exact pattern of capitalization you want to match.

5. If you want to perform a replace operation, press **Enter** or **Tab** and type the replacement text next to the Replace With option.

6. Press **F10**.

7. If a match is found, press **F10** to make the replacement. Press **F7** to look for the next occurrence. Press **Esc** to cancel the search.

   If no match is found, you see a message and the search and replace operation is cancelled.

To perform a search for part of a word

1. Press **F7**.

2. Press **PgDn** to display the advanced features.

3. Use the **Tab** key to select the Type option, and press the spacebar to choose Text.

4. Use the **Tab** key to select the Search for: option, and type the search phrase.

   Be sure to type the exact pattern of capitalization you want to match.

5. If you want to perform a replace operation, press **Enter** or **Tab** and type the replacement text next to the Replace With option.

6. Press **F10**.

7. If a match is found, press **F10** to make the replacement. Press **F7** to look for the next occurrence. Press **Esc** to cancel the search.

   If no match is found, you see a message and the search and replace operation is cancelled.

To perform a search for a pattern

1. Press **F7**.

2. Press **PgDn** to display the advanced features.

3. Use the **Tab** key to select the Type option, and press the Spacebar to choose Pattern.

4. Use the **Tab** key to select the Search for: option, and type the search phrase.

   You may use the 9, a, and ~ wildcards.

5. If you want to perform a replace operation, press **Enter** or **Tab** and type the replacement text next to the Replace With option.

   You cannot use wildcards in replacement phrases.

6. Press **F10**.

7. If a match is found, press **F10** to make the replacement. Press **F7** to look for the next occurrence. Press **Esc** to cancel the search.

   If no match is found, you see a message and the search and replace operation is cancelled.

To perform a forward or backward search

1. Press **F7**.

2. Press **PgDn** to display the advanced features.

3. Press **Tab** to select the Range option, and press the spacebar to choose To end or To beginning.

   Normally, Write searches the whole document. If you choose To end, Write searches only from the cursor to the end of the document. If you choose To beginning, Write searches from the cursor to the beginning of the document.

4. Use the **Tab** key to select the Search for: option, and type the search phrase.

   Be sure to type the exact pattern of capitalization you want to match.

5. If you want to perform a replace operation, press **Enter** or **Tab** and type the replacement text next to the Replace With option.

6. Press **F10**.

7. If a match is found, press **F10** to make the replacement. Press **F7** to look for the next occurrence. Press **Esc** to cancel the search.

   If no match is found, you see a message and the search and replace operation is cancelled.

To perform a search and replace operation with automatic replacement

1. Press **F7**.

2. Press **Tab** to select the Method option, and press the spacebar to choose Automatic or Fast Automatic.

   The Automatic option displays each substitution as it is being made, but Fast Automatic does not.

3. Use the **Tab** key to select the Search for: option, and type the search phrase.

   Be sure to type the exact pattern of capitalization you want to match.

4. Press **Enter** or **Tab** and type the replacement text next to the Replace With option.

5. Press **F10**.

   If no match is found, you see a message and the search and replace operation is cancelled.

To perform a search and replace operation that removes a word without replacing anything

1. Press **F7**.

2. Press **Tab** to select the Method option, and press the spacebar to choose Automatic or Fast Automatic.

3. Press **Tab** to select the Search for: option, and type the search phrase.

   Be sure to type the exact pattern of capitalization you want to match.

4. Press **Enter** or **Tab** and type two periods (..) next to the Replace With option.

5. Press **F10**.

   If no match is found, you see a message and the search and replace operation is cancelled.

Search Options

FILE

Purpose

Tailors a Search/Update operation to retrieve documents that meet your search criteria.

Notes

By default, Q&A assumes the AND operator when you type text or numbers to be matched in two or more fields. This search method is highly restrictive.

If you want, you can change the search logic so that the OR operator becomes the default temporarily. An OR search is less restrictive. A record need have only one of the criteria. However, OR makes it harder to pinpoint a search for one record.

You can also change the default operator to NOT. Q&A will retrieve all the records that do *not* contain the text or numbers you specify on the retrieval spec.

You can combine these choices in the following four ways:

- **DO/ALL** retrieves only those forms that meet all the search restrictions you specify.

- **DO/ANY** retrieves all the forms that meet at least one of the search restrictions you specify.

- **DO NOT/ALL** retrieves all forms that fail to meet at least one of the search restrictions you specify

- **DO NOT/ANY** retrieves any form that fails to meet all the search restrictions you specify.

To change from AND to OR logic

1. Choose **S**earch/Update from the File menu.

2. Type the name of the data base and press **Enter**.

3. Press **Ctrl-F7**.

4. Use the arrow keys to highlight ANY.

5. Press **F10**.

To choose NOT logic

1. Choose **S**earch/Update from the File menu.

2. Type the name of the database and press **Enter**.

3. Press **Ctrl-F7**.

4. Use the arrow keys to highlight DO NOT.

5. Press **F10**.

Search/Update

FILE

Purpose

Retrieves records that meet criteria you specify. In addition, provides an opportunity to edit, update, or add information on forms you've already filled out. You may also use Search/Update to delete unwanted records from the database.

Notes

The result of a search is a single record, a group of records that all meet criteria you specify, or the entire database. Once you have retrieved the record(s), you can edit the information, update the information, add more information, or delete the record.

By default, Q&A assumes the AND operator when you type text or numbers to be matched in two or more fields. This search method is highly restrictive.

Once you retrieve the records, you press **F10** and **F9** to browse through the records, one by one. To view up to 17 records at once in abbreviated form (Table View), press **F6**. To determine which fields appear in this display mode, see *Table View*.

To retrieve a single record

1. Choose **S**earch/Update from the File menu.

2. Type the name of the database and press **Enter**.

3. Type text that is unique to the data record you want to retrieve.

To make sure you retrieve just the record you want, type text or numbers to be matched in more than one field.

4. Press **F10** to display the record.

   Update or edit the record.

5. Press **Shift-F10** to save the changes and return to the File Menu.

To search for one or more records

1. Choose **S**earch/Update from the File menu.

2. Type the name of the data base and press **Enter**.

3. Type search restriction options in one or more fields to retrieve records selectively.

4. Press **F10** to display the records.

   Use **F9** and **F10** to go back and forth among the records you've retrieved.

5. Press **Shift-F10** to save your changes and return to the File Menu.

To retrieve all the records in the database

1. Choose **S**earch/Update from the File menu.

2. Type the name of the database and press **Enter**.

3. Leave the Retrieve Spec screen blank.

4. Press **F10** to display all the records.

   Use **F9** and **F10** to go back and forth among the records you've retrieved.

5. Press **Shift-F10** to save your changes and return to the File Menu.

To delete an unwanted data record

1. Choose **S**earch/Update from the File menu.

2. Type the name of the database and press **Enter**.

3. Type text that is unique to the data record you want to delete.

4. Press **F10** to display the record.

5 Press **F3**.

6.` Type **Y** to confirm the deletion.

7. Press **Shift-F10** to return to the File Menu.

To print the form displayed on the screen

1. Press **F2**.

2. Choose Print Options, if you want.

3. Press **F10** to start printing.

Search Restriction Options: All Information Types

Symbol	Function
x	Field must contain x.
=x	Field must contain x.
/x	Field can contain anything except x.
=	Field must be empty.
/=	Field must not be empty.

Search Restriction Options: All Information Types Except Yes/No Fields

Symbol	Explanation of example
x;y	Field must contain x or y.
x;y;z	Field must contain x, or y, or z.
>x	Number must be greater than x.
<x	Number must be less than x.
>=x	Number must be greater than or equal to x.
x..	Number must be greater than or equal to x.
..x	Number must be less than or equal to x.
<=x	Number must be less than or equal to x.
x..y	Number must be in x to y range.

>x..<y	Number must be greater than x and less than y.
MAXn	Retrieve records with 3 highest values in field.
MINn	Retrieve records with 3 lowest values in field.

Search Restriction Options: Text and Keyword Fields

Symbol	Explanation
~	Use to find words that sound alike.
?	Use to match any single character.
****	Use to match literal character .
..	To find anything from the dots to the end of the specification.
x..	Retrieves only if field begins with x.
..x	Retrieves only if field ends with x.
x..y	Retrieves only if field begins with x and ends with y.
..x..	Retrieves only if field includes x.
..x..y..z..	Retrieves only if field includes x, y, and z, in that order.

Search Restriction Options: Keyword Field Only

Symbol	Explanation
x;y;z	Field must contain x or y or z.
&x;y;z	Field must contain x and y and z.

Search Restriction Options: Special Search

Symbol	Explanation of example
..	Retrieves only those records that contain correctly formatted data.
/..	Retrieves only those records that do not contain correctly formatted data.
]	In date fields only, matches the following text.

Search/Update Function Keys

Key	Function
F1	Help
F2	Prints current form
Shift-F2	Macros
Ctrl-F2	Prints from current form to end of stack
F3	Deletes current record
F4	Delete from cursor to end of field
Shift-F4	Delete all characters in field
F5	Ditto current field from previous record
Shift-F5	Ditto previously viewed record
Ctrl-F5	Auto-type current date
Alt-F5	Auto-type current time
F6	Displays up to 17 records in 5-column table
F7	Go to Search/Update and display Retrieve Spec Screen
F8	Calculates
Shift-F8	Sets Calc mode
Ctrl-F8	Resets @NUMBER
F9	Save and display previous record
Shift-F9	Go to Customize spec screen
F10	Save and display a new, blank form
Shift-F10	Save record and exit

Set Global Options

FILE

Purpose

Choose Print Options for all the new print specs you create.

Notes

This command affects the output generated by the Print command in the File Menu, and produces printouts simply and quickly. For more complex printing, see *Report*.

You can choose the following print and page options for printouts:

- **Print Options** sets the route output; chooses manual or continuous paper feed, as well as chooses the bin from which paper is drawn (for multibin printers); chooses to offset the page by the number of characters you specify so there is room for binding; sends printer control codes to the printer to select such features as condensed printing; includes or omits field labels; prints more than one copy; prints more than one form per page; and prints more than one label across the page.

- **Define Page** For print output generated by the Print Forms command, you can choose to: specify a new page width, page length, and margins; specify how many characters per inch to print; and include headers and footers.

- **Single Form Print Defaults** This command displays the same Print Options screen just mentioned, but the choices you make apply to the single-form printing you initiate when you press F2 while adding or updating data.

- **Single Form Page Defaults** This command displays the same Print Options screen just mentioned, but the choices you make apply to the single-form printing you initiate when you press F2 while adding or updating data.

If you choose the Print Options and/or Define Page options, the choices you make affect all the new Print

Specs you create (but not old ones). For information on creating Print Specs, see *Design/Redesign a Spec*.

To change the print options defaults for all new print specs

1. Choose **P**rint from the File Menu.

2. Type the name of the database you want to customize.

3. Press **Enter**.

4. Choose **S**et Global Options.

5. To affect all new print specs, press **A** to select Change print options defaults. To affect single-form printing output with the F2 key, choose **C**hange single form print defaults.

6. Tab to the option you want to change. For fields that require you to type somthing, select the field with Tab and type a response.

7. Press **F10** to save the options you have selected.

To change the define page defaults for all new print specs

1. Choose **P**rint from the File Menu.

2. Type the name of the database you want to customize.

3. Press **Enter**.

4. Choose **S**et Global Options from the Global Options menu.

5. To affect all new print specs for this database, press **B** to select Change define page defaults. To affect single-form print output with the F2 key, press **D** to select Change single-form page defaults.

6. Tab to the option you want to change. For fields that require you to type somthing, select the field with Tab and type a response.

   You can type a header and/or footer that uses up to three lines.

7. Press **F10** to save the options you have selected.

Set Global Options

REPORT

Purpose

Redefines defaults for column headings and width, report format options, print options, and page definition options for all new report formats.

Notes

The Set Global Options menu displays these choices:

- **Set Column Headings/Width** enables you to type column headings and widths that differ from the labels in the database. Your choice affects all the new report formats you create for a database.

- **Set Format Options** enables you to choose new defaults for the automatic spacing between columns, the repetition of values in sorted columns, and the treatment of blank fields and column breaks. Your choices affect all the new report formats for all your databases.

- **Set Print Options** enables you to choose new print options for new report formats for all databases.

- **Set Page Options** enables you to choose new page definitions, including headers or footers with page numbers and automatic date and time, for the new report formats for all your databases.

The choices you make in Set Global Options do not affect report formats you have already created.

To change the column headings or width for all new reports for a particular database

1. Choose **R**eport from the Main Menu.

2. Choose **S**et Global Options.

3. Type the name of the data file for which you are designing the report.

4. Press **C** to select Set column headings/widths from the Global Options menu.

5. Type the column width followed by a colon, and then type the new column heading.

   To split the heading over two or more lines, type an exclamation point (!) where you want the split.

6. Repeat Step 5 for additional columns.

7. Press **F10** to save your work and continue.

To change the format options for all new report formats

1. Choose **R**eport from the Main Menu.

2. Choose **S**et Global Options.

3. Type the name of the data file for which you are designing the report.

4. Press **F** to select Set format options from the Global Options menu.

5. Press the **Tab** key to select the option you want to change.

6. Use the spacebar to choose the setting you want, and press **Enter**.

7. Repeat Steps 5 and 6 until you have chosen all the options you want.

8. Press **F10** to save your work and continue.

To change printing options for all new report formats

1. Choose **R**eport from the Main Menu.

2. Choose **S**et Global Options.

3. Type the name of the data file for which you are designing the report.

4. Press **P** to select Set print formats from the Global Options menu.

5. Press **Tab** to select the option you want to change.

   For information on these options, see *Print Options*.

6. Use the spacebar to choose the setting you want, and press **Enter**.

7. Repeat Steps 5 and 6 to choose all options.

8. Press **F10** to save your work and continue.

To change Define Page options for all new report formats

1. Choose **R**eport from the Main Menu.

2. Choose **S**et Global Options.

3. Type the name of the data file for which you are designing the report.

4. Press **D** to select Set page options from the Global Options menu.

5. Press **Tab** to select the Define Page option you want to change.

6. Type the new value or press the spacebar to select the option you want.

7. Press **Enter**.

8. Repeat Steps 5 through 7 to change additional items.

Set Global Options

WRITE

Purpose

Changes editing, printing, and page definition defaults for all Write documents you create.

Notes

The following list summarizes the options you can choose from the Set Global Options screen (the default settings are shown in boldface):

- **Set Editing Options**. From this screen, you can change many word processing defaults: default editing mode (**Overtype**, Insert); the default export type (**ASCII with CR**, ASCII without CR), ghost cursor that tracks the cursor's location on the tab ruler (**Yes**, No), Show margins on screen (**Yes**, No), Automatic backup created when the document is loaded (Yes, **No**), Decimal convention (**American**, European), Default tab settings (**5, 15, 25, 35** columns), Spacing between columns (.25").

- **Set Print Defaults** You choose From Page (**1**), To page (**9999**), Number of copies (**1**), Print offset (**0**), Line spacing (**Single**, Double, Envelope), Justify (Yes, **No**), Print to (**PtrA**, PtrB, PtrC, PtrD, PtrE, DISK), Type of paper feed (Manual, Continuous, Bin1, Bin2, Bin 3, Lhd), Number of columns (**1**, 2, 3, 4, 5, 6, 7, 8), Printer control codes (blank), Name of Merge File (blank).

- **Change Page Defaults** You choose Left margin (**10** columns), Right margin (**68** columns from left edge of page), Top margin (**6** lines from top), Bottom margin (**6** lines from bottom), Page width (**78** columns), Page length (**66** lines), Characters per inch (**10**, 12, 15, 17), Begin headers/footers on page **1**, Begin page numbering with page # **1**.

The changes you make in any of these screens affect all the Write documents you create.

To set the editing options

1. Choose **U**tilities from the Write Menu.

2. Choose **S**et Global Options.

3. Choose Set **E**diting options.

4. Choose the field you want to change.

5. Select the option you want, or type the value.

6. Repeat Steps 4 and 5 until you have chosen the defaults you want.

7. Press **F10** to save your choices.

To change the print defaults

1. Choose **U**tilities from the Write Menu.

2. Choose **S**et Global Options.

3. Choose Change **P**rint Defaults.

4. Choose the field you want to change.

5. Select the option you want, or type the value.

6. Repeat Steps 4 and 5 until you have chosen the defaults you want.

7. Press **F10** to save your choices.

To change the page defaults

1. Choose **U**tilities from the Write Menu.

2. Choose **S**et Global Options.

3. Choose Change Page **D**efaults.

4. Choose the field you want to change.

5. Use the spacebar to select the option you want, or type the value.

6. Repeat Steps 4 and 5 until you have chosen the defaults you want.

7. Press **F10** to save your choices.

Set Global Options

UTILITIES

Purpose

Sets defaults for the DOS location of Q&A document and database files, command execution, and network identification.

Notes

Keep your database and document files in directories other than Q&A's. That way, you can't accidentally erase Q&A files while performing cleanup operations.

After you learn Q&A, choose the option that executes commands after you press the command's letter. By default, pressing the command letter only highlights the command in the menu. You have to press Enter to execute the command. After you change the default, pressing the letter executes the command, saving you a keystroke.

To change the default document and database directories

1. Use DOS to create subdirectories within Q&A's directory for databases and documents.

   If Q&A is in C:\QA, create subdirectories called C:\QA\DOCS and C:\QA\DATA.

2. Start Q&A and choose **U**tilities from the Main Menu.

3. Type the name of the document directory and press **Enter**.

4. Type the name of the database directory and press **Enter**.

To change the default command execution mode

1. Choose **U**tilities from the Main Menu.

2. Press **Tab** to select the Automatic Execution field.

3. Press the spacebar to select **Y**es.

4. Press **F10** to save your choices.

Set Initial Values

FILE

Purpose

Predefines values or text for information blanks so that these values appear automatically on new forms.

Note

Use this option to fill in new forms with the most likely value or text. If it isn't correct, the user can change it when adding new forms.

To access the Customize Menu

1. Choose **F**ile from the Main Menu.

2. Choose **D**esign File.

3. Type the name of the database you want to customize.

4. Press **Enter**.

5. Choose **C**ustomize a File.

6. Press **Enter** to confirm the file name.

To set initial values

1. Choose Set **I**nitial Values from the Customize Menu.

2. Type the initial value in the field.

3. Type more initial values.

   To cancel the initial value you typed in a field, place the cursor in the field and press **F3**.

4. Press **F10** to save and continue.

Initial Values Spec Screen Function Keys

Key	Function
F1	How to set initial values
F3	Cancel initial values spec in a field
F10	Continue

Single Form Printing

FILE

Purpose

Prints the form displayed on the screen.

Note

You can print the form displayed on-screen or print all the forms you added during a data-entry session.

To choose print options and page defaults for printing single forms, see *Set Global Options*.

To print the form displayed on the screen

1. Press **F2**.

2. Choose Print Options, if you want.

3. Press **F10** to start printing.

To print all the forms you add in a data-entry session

1. Press **Ctrl-Home**.

2. Press **Ctrl-F2**.

3. Press **F10**.

Soft Hyphens

WRITE

Purpose

Inserts an optional hyphen, which Q&A uses only if breaking the word improves the appearance of the line.

Note

Use soft hyphens to make sure that especially long words do not leave unsightly gaps in your document.

To add a soft hyphen:

1. Place the cursor on the character before which you want the soft hyphen to be inserted.

2. Press **Alt-F6**.

Sort

FILE

Purpose

Arranges records according to defined sorting criteria.

Notes

By default, Q&A keeps your records in the order you entered them. You may want to sort them so you can browse through them for updating purposes.

You can define two or more sort levels. The first level sort (primary level) arranges all the records in ascending or descending order. The second level sort deals with records whose order can't be determined by the first level sort.

After you sort the records, you may edit, update, add more data, or delete the records, just as you do in Search/Update.

To sort all the records in the database

1. Choose **S**earch/Update from the File menu.

2. Type the name of the data base and press **Enter**.

3. Press **F8**.

4. Place the cursor in the primary sort field and type **1**.

   To choose an ascending sort, type **AS**. To choose a descending sort, type **DS**.

5. Place the cursor in the next sort field and type a number that is one whole number larger than the previous one.

   In the second field, you would type **2**. Be sure to type **AS** or **DS**.

6. Repeat Step 5 using increasingly higher numbers for each additional sort criterion.

7. Press **F10** to start the sort.

Search/Update Function Keys

Key	*Funciton*
F1	Help
F2	Prints current form
Shift-F2	Macros
Ctrl-F2	Prints from current form to end of stack
F3	Deletes current record
F4	Deletes from cursor to end of field
Shift-F4	Deletes all characters in field
F5	Ditto current field from previous record
Shift-F5	Ditto previously viewed record

Ctrl-F5	Auto-type current date
Alt-F5	Auto-type current time
F6	Displays up to 17 records in 5-column table
F7	Goes to Search/Update and displays Retrieve Spec Screen
F8	Calculates
Shift-F8	Sets Calc mode
Ctrl-F8	Resets @NUMBER
F9	Save and display previous record
Shift-F9	Go to Customize spec screen
F10	Save and display a new, blank form
Shift-F10	Save record and exit

Speed Up Searches

FILE

Purpose

Creates a presorted index of frequently-searched fields so that large databases are searched faster. You can also use this command to make sure that a field contains a unique entry (not duplicated on any other record) or a non-unique entry (a response that already exists elsewhere in the database).

Notes

Speeding up searches makes sense only for large databases. You can index up to 115 fields. However, each index takes up disk space.

If you have created a database in which records are identified by some unique information (such as a social security or employee number), use this command to make sure a field contains a unique entry.

If you want to limit responses in a field to information that has been entered previously, use this command to make sure a field contains a *non*-unique entry (in other words, an entry that has been used elsewhere).

To access the Customize Menu

1. Choose **F**ile from the Main Menu.

2. Choose **D**esign File.

3. Type the name of the database you want to customize.

4. Press **Enter**.

5. Choose **C**ustomize a File.

6. Press **Enter** to confirm the file name.

To mark a field for automatic indexing

1. Choose **S**peed-up Searches from the Customize Menu.

2. Place the cursor in the field you want indexed.

3. Type **S**.

4. Repeat steps for additional fields.

5. Press **F10**.

To make sure a field contains a unique entry

1. Choose **S**peed-up Searches from the Customize Menu.

2. Place the cursor in the field you want indexed.

3. Type **SU**.

4. Repeat steps for additional fields.

5. Press **F10**.

To make sure a field contains a non-unique entry

1. Choose **S**peed-up Searches from the Customize Menu.

2. Place the cursor in the field you want indexed.

3. Type **SE**.

4. Repeat step for additional fields.

5. Press **F10**.

Summary Functions

REPORT

Purpose

Returns column totals, subtotals, averages, and other statistics so that these values can be used in derived column formulas.

Notes

In a database report, you use summary functions in reports to perform calculations based on totals taken from other columns. These summary functions can be used *only* in the Derived Columns screen.

Function	Explanation
@TOTAL(n)	Returns grand total of values in column n
@TOTAL(n,m)	Returns subtotal of values in column n where a break occurs in column m
@AVERAGE(n)	Returns grand average of values in column n
@AVERAGE(n,m)	Returns subaverage of values in column n where a break occurs in column m
@COUNT(n)	Returns grand total count of values in column n
@COUNT(n,m)	Returns subcount of values in column n where a break occurs in column m
@MINIMUM(n)	Returns lowest value in column n
@MINIMUM(n,m)	Returns lowest value in column n where a break occurs in column m
@MAXIMUM(n)	Returns highest value in column n
@MAXIMUM(n,m)	Returns highest value in column n where a break occurs in column m

Table View

FILE

Purpose

Displays up to 17 records at a time in Search/Update.

Notes

You see each data record expressed as a row on the screen, with five columns containing the first 20 characters of five fields. You can only view these records. Special cursor movement keys aid you in navigating the Table View screens.

By default, the five Table View columns contain the first five fields in your database design. You can override this default setting and tell Q&A which fields you want displayed in Table View.

To display a Table View of the entire database:

1. Choose **S**earch/Update from the File menu.

2. Type the name of the database and press **Enter**.

3. Leave the Retrieve Spec screen blank.

4. Press **F10** to display the records.

5. Press **F6** to display the Table View.

6. To display a record, use the arrow keys to highlight the record and press **F10**.

Cursor movement keys in Table View

Key	Cursor Movement
Up arrow or **F9**	Moves to previous row.
Down Arrow or **Spacebar**	Moves to next row.
Home	Moves to top of current display screen.
End	Moves to bottom of current display screen.
Ctrl-Home	Moves to first row in table.

Ctrl-End	Moves to last row in table.
PgUp	Moves to previous 17 rows.
PgDn	Moves to next 17 rows.

To select the fields that appear in the Table View mode
1. Choose **S**earch/Update from the File menu.
2. Type the name of the database and press **Enter**.
3. Leave the Retrieve Spec screen blank.
4. Press **F10** to display the records.
5. Press **Shift-F6** to display the Table View Spec screen.
6. Place the cursor in the field you want to appear in Column 1, and type **1**.
7. Place the cursor in the field you want to appear in Column 2, and type **2**.
8. Continue until you have selected five fields.
9. Press **F10** to see Table View in customized form.

Tabs

FILE, WRITE

Purpose
Overrides the default tab stops

Notes
You can change these settings for a database or a document, and the changes are saved with it. You also can create decimal tab stops. With decimal tabs, characters are entered flush right until you type a period (decimal point); then the characters align normally.

To change the default tab settings for all documents, see *Set Global Options*.

To change tabs
1. Press **F8** (Options).

2. Choose **S**et Tabs.

3. Press the right- or left-arrow keys to position the cursor on the tab line.

4. Type **T** for a flush left tab or **D** for a decimal tab.

   To delete an existing tab stop, place the cursor on the tab and press **Del**.

5. Repeat Steps 3 and 4 to set all the tabs you want.

6. Press **F10**.

Temporary Margins

WRITE

Purpose

Temporarily indents text from the left and right margins.

Notes

The left margin change begins on the line below the current cursor position, and the right margin change begins on the current line. You see right and left brackets on the ruler line that mark the temporary margins.

If you are indenting text in an existing document, the indentation takes effect for the current paragraph only. If you are typing new text, however, the indentation continues to the next paragraph. To restore the normal margins, you must press **F6** and choose **C**lear.

To indent text left and right

1. Place the cursor on the column in which you want the left or right indent to occur.

2. Press **F6**.

3. Type **L** for left margin or **R** for right margin.

4. Type the text to be indented.

To remove temporary indentations

1. Place the cursor within the indented text.

2. Press **F6**.

3. Type **C** to Clear the temporary margins.

Text Enhancements

WRITE

Purpose

Formats characters with boldface, italics, subscript, superscript, underline, strikeout, and printer fonts.

Notes

For information on using fonts, see *Font Assignments* and *Fonts*.

To choose text enhancements

1. Type the text you want enhanced.

2. Move the cursor to the first character of the text you want enhanced.

3. Press **Shift-F6**.

4. Choose **B**oldface, **U**nderline, **I**talic, **S**ubscript, Su**P**erscript, **X** Strikeout, or **F**ont

5. Highlight all the text you want enhanced.

6. Press **F10**.

To restore normal text, highlight the text press **Shift-F6** and choose **R**egular. Press **F10**.

Type/Edit

WRITE

Purpose

Creates a new document or permits editing of the document currently in memory.

Note

To edit a document on disk, use **G**et before choosing
Type/Edit.

Type/Edit Function Keys

Key	*Function*
F1	Displays Help Menu.
Shift-F1	Checks spelling.
Ctrl-F1	Checks word spelling.
F2	Prints document.
Shift-F2	Defines macro.
Ctrl-F2	Prints block.
F3	Deletes block.
Ctrl-F3	Counts words, lines, and paragraphs.
F4	Deletes word.
Shift-F4	Deletes line.
F5	Copies block.
Shift-F5	Moves block.
Ctrl-F5	Copies block to file.
Alt-F5	Moves block to file.
F6	Sets temporary margins.
Shift-F6	Enhances text.
Ctrl-F6	Defines page.
Alt-F6	Adds soft hyphen.
F7	Performs search and replace.

Shift-F7	Restores deletion or makes multiple copies.
Ctrl-F7	Goes to a specific page or line.
F8	Displays Options Menu.
Shift-F8	Saves.
Ctrl-F8	Turns on Export.
Alt-F8	Prints mailing labels.
F9	Scrolls down.
Shift-F9	Scrolls up.
Ctrl-F9	Displays font assignments.
Alt-F9	Turns on Calculate.
F10	Continues.

Index